CABARET

CABARET
Lisa Appignanesi

Grove Press, Inc.
New York

The original Cabaret Voltaire poster designed by Marcel Slodki. Kunsthaus Zurich.

Originally published in Great Britain in 1975 by Studio Vista

First published in the United States in 1976 by Universe Books

This revised and updated edition is published in the United States in 1984 by Grove Press, Inc., 196 West Houston Street, New York, NY, 10014

First Evergreen Edition 1984
First Printing 1984
ISBN: 0-394-62177-8
Library of Congress Catalog Card Number: 84-47500

Printed in Great Britain
5 4 3 2 1

Contents

Acknowledgements

Much of the material of this book is based on living memory and a number of people have given me generously of their time and knowledge, either in interview and correspondence or by helping me with photographic and textual sources. My thanks go to Klaus Budzinski, whose works on cabaret are invaluable documents in the field, Dr Tilman Spengler, the late Hans and Lillie Hess, Wolfgang Roth, Egon Larsen, Hannah Norbert, Mary Gerold-Tucholsky, Gertrude Heartfield, Werner Finck, John Willett, Michael Kustow, M. Leclerc of the Musée de vieux Montmartre, Massimo Prampolini, and M. Roland Liot, the photographer, for his excellent work in reproducing French posters, photos and paintings.

Grateful thanks go to the following for use of extracts and quotations: Associated Book Publishers Ltd, for 'The Soldier's Song' from Bertolt Brecht's *Collected Plays*, vol. I, © 1970 Methuen & Co. Ltd; Macmillan, London and Basingstoke, and Abner Stein, New York, for the extract from *Lenny Bruce* by J. Cohen; Mrs Blandine Ebinger for Friedrich Holländer's 'Groschenlied'; Jonathan Cape Ltd for Patrick Bridgwater's translation of 'The Other Possibility' from *Let's Face It* by Erich Kästner; Atrium Verlag, Zurich, for the extracts from 'Surabaya-Johnny II' in *Kästner für Erwachsene*; Die Arche Verlag, Zurich, and Walter Mehring, for the poems by Walter Mehring; the Akademie der Künste der DDR for Erich Mühsam's 'Der Revoluzzer', and John Burgess for his translation, taken from *Toller* by Tancred Dorst; the Henssel Verlag for Joachim Ringelnatz's 'Und einmal steht es neben dir', Berlin 1974; the Kurt Tucholsky Archiv and Rowohlt Verlag for the poems by Kurt Tucholsky; R. Piper & Co. Verlag for Karl Valentin's 'Tingeltangel' from *Gesammelte Werke* © R. Piper & Co. Verlag, Munich 1961; the Aufbau Verlag, Berlin, for 'The Carnival Parade of the Republic' by Erich Weinert.

Particular thanks are due to Dorothea Gotfurt who kindly volunteered to do several song translations for this book, to Tristram Holland for her untiring help in picture research, to Stephen Adamson and Jenny Towndrow of Studio Vista and Nick Hern of Methuen for their editorial assistance. Finally I would like to thank Tony Allen, Richard Strange and Kathy Acker and particularly my colleagues at the ICA, John Ashford and Michael Morris, for all their help in preparing this new up-dated version of the book; and my son Joshua for his patience in putting up with a writing mum.

Ladies and Gentlemen,
Mesdames et Messieurs,
Meine Damen und Herren,
introducing . . .

Cabaret In popular usage the word most generally conjures up visions of seedy strip joints on dank, dimly lit, city streets, or alternately, nightclubs where the exorbitant price of drinks is rarely linked to the meagre stage fare. To these images the film *Cabaret* has added a grim aura of Weimarian decadence and a hint of satire which is all too quickly lost in sentimentality. In effect, these versions of cabaret are only the impoverished distant relatives of the literary cabaret which emerged in France in the last century and blossomed into a unique medium for political and cultural satire in the German *Kabarett* of the twenties and early thirties. They share with the artistic cabaret only the presence of spectacle and an intimate space in which people can smoke and talk, eat and drink.

The cabaret inherits its name from the French wine cellar or tavern. As early as Villon's day such cabarets served as performance locales, either because tipsy guests spontaneously joined in sing-song, or because an enterprising host, wanting to attract more customers, allowed his premises to be used by strolling players, balladeers, jugglers, and the whole retinue of out-of-season carnival personalities. The two related forms of artistic cabaret, which were to emerge some centuries later, are already here in germ – cabaret as a meeting place for artists where quasi-improvisational performance takes place among peers, and cabaret as an intimate, small-scale, but intellectually ambitious revue.

In the latter half of the nineteenth century, the song, or *chanson*, became the principle form of entertainment provided by the French cafés and bistros. It is difficult to imagine now the full importance of the song as a medium of public communication in those radio- and television-free days. Not only was the chanson a love lyric or mood piece which entertained, but it could function as a reporting vehicle – a performed alternative to the newspaper, which because of its dependence on machinery and finance, was largely controlled by the ruling class. As such, the *chanson* was one of the few means by which the people could record their daily history and publicly voice their reactions to contemporary events. A people's version of the newspaper, passed on orally in streets, cafés, meetings and taverns, the song could spoof or ridicule authority and act as a rallying call. Thus it came to serve as a democratic and satirical weapon for criticism and protest.

Here, for example, is a satirical song called 'The Expulsion' by Mac-Nab. It was written during the height of anarchistic activity in

9

A Montmarte chansonnier. Bibliothèque historique de la ville de Paris.

The 'Taverne des Truands' or Vagrants Tavern. Paris in the *belle époque*. Bibliothèque historique de la ville de Paris.

10

Third Republic France. The singer ironically takes on the voice of an anarchist in order to express a protest against the possible return of royalty to republican France. Meanwhile, he airs a variety of grievances which result in his wanting to expel just about everyone from the country.

> *Moi, j'vas vous dire la vérité,*
> *Les princ' il est capitalisse,*
> *Et l'travailleur est exploité,*
> *C'est ça la mort du socialisse.*
>
> *Les princ' c'est pas tout. Plus d'aurés,*
> *Plus d'gendarmes, plus d'militaires,*
> *Plus d'richards à lambris dorés,*
> *Qui boit la sueur de prolétaire.*
>
> *Enfin qu'tout l'mond' soye expulsé,*
> *Il rest'ra plus qu' les anarchisses.*
>
> Me, I'm going to give you the truth,
> The princes, they are capitalist,
> And the worker is exploited,
> And that's the death of the socialist.
>
> Besides princes, no more lordly ones,
> No more cops, no more military men,
> No more filthy rich in their mansions,
> Who drink the sweat of the proletarian.
>
> Finally when everyone's been thrown out,
> There'll be only anarchists about.

In a few lines, this song voices the people's protest against their 'rulers' and simultaneously undermines anarchistic politics.

As the bistro or café with its solitary singer took on grander proportions and received official permission to use costumes and props, it grew into the *café-concert*, the native French form of what was to become the music-hall towards the end of the century. These *cafés-concerts* generally catered to a large audience; they were often situated – weather permitting – in the open air, and would sometimes house full-scale bands. Their prime concern was entertainment. While the satirical or protest song might accidentally be part of their programme, this more aggressive form of the *chanson* found its more natural home in the intimate cabaret.

Growing out of the *café-concert*, the cabaret was from its modern inception in 1881 immediately a more intellectual and self-consciously artistic form, though laughter and entertainment were of its essence. Its birth was sparked by a literary society known as the *Hydropathes*, which met weekly so that writers and poets could perform their works for one another – whether poetry, sung lyric, monologue or short sketch. The increasing size of the Hydropathes' gatherings testified to the fact that artists wanted to meet in this way in order to exchange work and ideas with one another. This, together with the

11

artists' adoption of the popular satirical or protest song as a principal mode of expression, were the initial ingredients which went into the making of the cabaret.

From then on the cabaret was marked by these two elements. It emerged either as a laboratory, a testing ground for young artists who often deliberately advertised themselves as an avant-garde, or as the satirical stage of contemporaneity, a critically reflective mirror of topical events, morals, politics and culture. In the best instances, it was both. Walking the tightrope between the stage proper and the variety show, the cabaret defined an independent territory for itself. A flexible medium – with its impromptu stage, setting and pro-gramme – it shifted its focus with the times, without ever on the whole losing its rebellious wit or dissident, innovative nature.

Given this flexibility and insistence on contemporaneity, it is difficult to generalize about the actual content of a typical cabaret programme. If the given is said to be an essentially unrelated series of say fifteen acts – including song, monologue, sketches, poetry and dance – then this standard can be contradicted by cabarets which emphasized one form over another; or had no formal programme and consisted of improvised acts by participant members; or others which concentrated on, say, hour-length plays preceded and followed by song or satirical monologue. Apart from its satirical and avant-garde emphasis what remain more or less consistent in cabaret and allow it to be defined as a distinct form, are its structural elements: a small stage and smallish audience and an ambience of talk and smoke, where the relationship between performer and spectator is one at once of intimacy and hostility, the nodal points of participation and provocation. The cabaret performer plays directly to his audience, breaking down the illusory fourth wall of traditional theatre. There is never any pretence made of an identity existing between actor and role. Rather, as in Brechtian drama, the performer remains a perfor-mer, no matter what he is enacting.

This genuine historical form of cabaret – together with its writers, performers, makers and the contemporary issues they confronted – is what the following pages describe. Since instances of cabaret are many, I have concentrated on only some of its principal manifestations in the key periods of its history. Since much of the cabaret's particular genius is devoted to topical satire and the lively, witty repartee be-tween performers and audience, I have tried to sketch in the con-temporary issues – socio-political and artistic – together with some-thing of the atmosphere of the time and the local setting. For any gross generalizations, I plead cabaretistic license.

Where songs and poems, many of them full of pungent street dialect, have not yet been rendered into English by poets capable of punning and turning a couplet far better than myself, I have in most instances presented the original together with an all but literal translation. As for the difficulty of rendering the vitality of live performance, of capturing piercing wit and laughter which is of the essence of cabaret, I can only urge readers to frequent one of the numerous venues which have opened in recent years where cabaret lives again. The following

12

merely seeks to outline the nature and value of a form of performance which can span the intellectual, the artistic and the popular, while providing a vehicle for living satire.

So, ladies and gentlemen, the cabaret . . .

Poster advertising the latest variety spectacle at the café-concert *Les Ambassadeurs* by Jules Cheret, 1884. Bibliothèque historique de la ville de Paris.

Le CHAT NOIR (Ronde)

Paroles du Ch.‌ Du FRESNEL
Musique de E. FEAUTRIER

Le Chat noir a grande moustache, Les grif-fes que son long poil cache

Sont des ser-rures de pri-sons, Et ses yeux verts sont deux ti-sons...

REFRAIN

Gare! à son pas-sa-ge, Bé-hé, soyez sa-ge. Autour du manoir Rôde le chat noir.

Le chat noir a grande moustache,
Les griffes que son long poil cache
Sont des serrures de prisons,
Et ses yeux verts sont deux tisons.

Le chat noir, fière sentinelle,
Lance l'éclair de sa prunelle;
Et malgré vent, neige ou grésil,
Il ne quitte pas son fusil.

Le chat noir, sans valet, ni page,
Quand les enfants font du tapage,
Arquepince les scélérats,
Comme les souris et les rats.

Le chat noir, à minuit, s'attable.
Il est gourmand et redoutable ;
Car il mange à la croque au sel
Tout méchant, fille ou jouvencel.

Le chat noir, quand il fait sa ronde,
Que la tête soit brune ou blonde,
Met dans son sac, sans examen,
Les méchants qu'il trouve en chemin.

Le chat noir, qui, bon diable en somme,
A juré de vivre en saint homme,
Ne commettra plus de méfaits
Quand les enfants seront parfaits.

Le chat noir se fera notaire
Trois jours avant d'aller en terre;
C'est pour finir paisiblement

Mais quelle sera la semaine
Qui verra sa griffe inhumaine
Gratter à l'huis du paradis?
— C'est celle des quatre jeudis!

Le chat noir est un gars solide
Qui n'a pas l'air d'un invalide;
Et les gens qui l'ont vu courir
Disent qu'il ne doit pas mourir

Paris 1881:
Cabaret is Born

A black cat placing a disdainful paw on an obliterated goose – such was the emblem of the first cabaret, and its originators were quick to suggest to us that this graceful, magical cat, born from the pages of Edgar Allan Poe, represents art; its unworthy prey, the sullen, squawking, silly bourgeois.

The first cabaretists gave birth to an eclectic cat. A cat who could sing, recite, dance, show shadow plays, write music, lyrics, farce, and above all, perform. A cat at once a revolutionary and a royalist, a mystic and a teller of broad tales, a lover of the gruesome macabre and the sentimental romantic – contradictions which could only be and were, indeed, resolved in the spirit of satirical laughter.

It is 1881. The Commune is ten years dead. Baron Haussmann's mammoth feat of reconstructing the face of Paris is complete – apart from his own ironically unfinished Boulevard Haussmann. Spacious boulevards and magnificent squares have replaced winding cobbled streets. The reasons for this grand architectural surgery – to hinder the building of insurrectionist barricades, to facilitate the movement of state troops and the firing of cannons – are all but forgotten. Paris

Opposite
One of the many French ballads about the legendary 'Black Cat'. Here he appears as a figure who punishes disobedient children. Musée du vieux Montmartre.

'*Jalousie féline*' Drawing in coloured inks by Adolphe Willette, 1888. The black cat appears here in a sexual light, as he does in much of Willette's work. Musée du vieux Montmartre.

Boulevard Clichy, the base of Montmartre, at the turn of the century. Bibliothèque historique de la ville de Paris.

stands transformed, a glittering world capital, and the Third Republic enjoys peace and economic prosperity. Anarchist bombs, political scandals and internal dissent are not to threaten its foundations for several years.

Yet a leading Paris newspaper welcomes in the New Year with this startling headline: 'Here lies 1880. The Year of Obscenity'. A strange epitaph for a time of apparent political calm and burgeoning economic activity in the bourgeois sector. But the streets are filled with beggars, urchins, ragpickers, prostitutes and thieves, as well as with the carriages of the wealthy. And the abundant newspapers prefer to offer their readers morbidly naturalistic tales — with sententious addenda, of course — about the lives of the former rather than the latter.

This moralizing, hypocritical fascination with the seamiest aspects of low life, propagated by the press, marked an extension and decline from the literary naturalism of Emile Zola. Such journalistic exploitations of misery underscore the fact that the borderline between crass sensationalism, pornography, and serious examination of the state of society had all but disappeared. The above headline was carried in revulsion.

Rodolphe Salis, with a few members of the Hydropathes society, took a farther-reaching step. He set up the first artistic cabaret. An initial aspect of this new genre's importance was to introduce satire into the cult of naturalism, to shock the middle-class spectator into a realization that his respectable values were merely a thin veneer hiding a lust for the sewer which he had himself partially helped to create.

Salis chose Montmartre as the Chat Noir's headquarters, then an outlying area which still retained its country character and its famous landmarks, the windmills. Winding dirt roads studded with vineyards, bistros, the occasional cow, chicken or donkey, led up this 'mount of the martyrs' to the squat multi-cupolaed pilgrimmage centre, Sacré Coeur, built just a few years previously on the site of one of the bloodier Communards' confrontations. Montmartre's population then consisted of the *canaille*, the rabble, a term they proudly applied to themselves and waved matador-like under the noses of the bourgeoisie. Criminals, the *apaches* of the Parisian frontier, pimps and their

16

'The elevated school of M. Emile Zola'. A satirical view of Emile Zola by Sapeck. The banner reads: 'Here anything goes from trotters to snout.' From cover of *Tout-Paris*, the one-time *Hydropathe* magazine, 1880. Musée du vieux Montmartre.

ladies, the poor, workers employed and unemployed – that whole hierarchy of social outcasts who were the very subjects of naturalist documentation – congregated in Montmartre. Salis, like other artists, had moved to this slightly treacherous environment because he could not afford the rising costs of the Latin Quarter. But the creation of the Chat Noir once and for all united in the public imagination the *canaille* with their spiritual kin, the members of the literary and artistic bohemia.

Rodolphe Salis, Baron de la Tour de Naintre, the son of a rich brewer, was a sometime painter, sometime poet. Above all else, however, Salis was a great publicist and inventor of artistic schemes. Latter-day member of the Hydropathes, he also founded l'Ecole vibrante, which aimed 'to fraternize Art with Literature', and followed that with the Ecole iriso-subversive de Chicago, which sought to prevent the encroachment of the Germans upon America.

The Chat Noir was initially a very modest undertaking. Poets, composers, writers, and painters, who were Salis's friends, would gather in his new Montmartre quarters and chat, read and perform their works for one another. The very 'club' or closed nature of the gatherings ensured that word of their existence would soon spread,

17

especially as the sounds which issued from the building until late in the evening provoked passers-by to wonder and complain, and upon occasion to intrude forcibly.

Salis then had the brilliant idea of serving drink to 'those who earned their thirst artistically', and since outsiders from the establishment Quartier Latin as well as from the immediate area insisted, of opening his doors to a select public once a week. He decorated his locale cheaply but artistically: sketches and paintings by thirsty artists including a wall-size oil by Adolphe Willette entitled *Parce Domine*, a symbolic saga of life and death in the carnival atmosphere of Montmartre. Then there were medieval arms, church candelabra, old doors, and Louis XIII furniture. When he realized that one nook of the room was so dank and narrow that no one wished to sit there, Salis decided to turn this fault into an advantage. With great ingenuity he called this corner 'The Institute'. He had waiters dressed in academicians' robes serve there, and suggested that only those who lived by the intellect could penetrate this élite sanctuary. The Institute soon expanded into the shop next door and became the trade mark of the Chat Noir.

The programme offered by the Chat Noir in its early years was unstructured. It functioned on the principle of surprise. Improvisational spontaneity, emphasized by the fact that creators themselves performed, was one of its major attractions. On any given night Emile Goudeau might be there reciting from his *Fleurs du Bitume*, asphalt flowers which reeked of city streets. Wielding a spoon rather than a

18

baton, Claude Debussy might be directing a choir. Then Maurice Mac-Nab, the genius of the macabre ballad, whose gallows humour sent shudders down the bourgeois spine, might deliver a few chansons, only to be followed by that other regular, Jules Jouy. Jouy, an active contributor to the revolutionary papers, *Cri du Peuple* and *Parti Ouvrier*, was one of the few participants of the Chat Noir actually to come from the people. His renowned songs provided a terse commentary on socio-political events, defying the Chat Noir public and calling his comrades to arms.

> *Patrons! tas d'Héliogabales,*
> *D'effroi saisis*
>
> *Quand vous tomberez sous nos balles,*
> *Chair à fusils,*
> *Pour que chaque chien sur vos trognes*
> *Pisse à l'écart.*
> *Nous leur laisserons vos charognes . . .*

> Bosses, you Heliogabuli,
> You will be seized by fear
>
> When you fall beneath our bullets,
> Flesh for rifles,
> Every dog will piss on your bloated faces
> In solitary places.
> We will leave them your carrion . . .

The original Chat Noir cabaret, Bibliothèque historique de la ville de Paris.

When the members of the Paris establishment ventured into the dark, muddy streets of Montmartre and through the doors of the Chat Noir, they knew they were coming to be insulted. Salis would welcome his guests with stiffly formal bows and mock salutations of 'Your Excellency', or 'Your esteemed Electoral Highnesses'. Contempt would reek from his fingertips as ever-increasing prices were paid for drinks. Many of the songs or poems performed were based on a parody of middle-brow culture. Subjects might be similar, but their treatment was infused with a cynical irony which precluded any possibility of sentimental effusion or self-righteous moralistic captioning.

The Chat Noir artists identified with the people in their immediate Montmartre environment. They lived, in some cases, as the people did; and by depicting the lives of the people in their verse, sung or spoken, by using their speech rhythms as well as their forms, these artists raised popular culture into an art which was to influence the literary mainstream – some of whose very makers were sitting in the cabaret's chairs. The Chat Noir public left revitalized by the critical impact.

In 1882, Salis launched a magazine also called *Chat Noir* which duplicated the goings-on and the spirit of the cabaret. It contained graphic work by Steinlen, Adolphe Willette, the poster artist Caran d'Ache and Forain; the satirical sketches of that famous methodical absurdist, Alphonse Allais; songs, poetry and commentary. Goudeau

The various possibilities of Paris night life, as seen by Jules Dépaquit in *Le Rire*, 1895. Courtesy the British Library.

was its editor for several years and was followed by Allais, and the journal was one of the brightest cornerstones of *la belle époque*.

Salis launched a peculiarly eccentric political campaign with this new publicity vehicle. The platform was the separation of Montmartre from the state. 'What is Montmartre? Nothing. What should it be? Everything.' Needless to say, Salis's campaign did not win him a seat, but it did succeed in drawing more and more artists to Montmartre, this *cerveau du monde*, and ever larger crowds to the Chat Noir.

It was time to move, not only because the cabaret was filled to overflowing. Some of the rougher members of Montmartre's teeming night life did not take too kindly to Salis's well-clad clientele and several assaults on the Chat Noir had already taken place. Salis had managed with aplomb more or less to incorporate these eruptions into the surprise sequence of the cabaret programme and this had added to the Chat Noir's attraction. However, when one of his waiters was stabbed and he himself badly mauled, a move was imminent. But no move on the part of the Chat Noir could be ordinary.

In the wake of Victor Hugo's mammoth funeral procession in 1885, a theatrical spectacle in which all Paris participated, Montmartre held its own only slightly less grand march. In the light of the moon, the cabaretists, each holding some piece of the old Chat Noir, danced, filed, and sang the length of the Boulevard de Rochechouart to their new headquarters on the rue Victor Massé. Drums, fifes, and violins accompanied the procession, headed by two Swiss guards in full regalia. Next came Salis in his prefect's costume; two 'hunters' carrying the black cat banner with its insignia, 'Montjoye et Montmartre'; four halberdiers bearing Willette's giant *Parce Domine*. Only when all of Montmartre had joined in the joyous *Marseillaise* of the Chat Noir was the move considered complete.

The new Chat Noir got under way after some initial problems with the new neighbours – quieter, but petitioning – and confrontations with the local police which were only resolved when Salis sought the help of one of his best clients, General Pittié at the Elysée Palace. For the next twelve years it was the gayest focal point of the Paris night life and avant-garde. Maupassant, Huysmans, Villier de l'Isle Adam, and Théodore de Banville were amongst its illustrious guests, not to mention the notorious Général Boulanger[1], several Paris mayors, and quite frequently the Prince of Wales, under pseudonym, of course.

Salis had his Parisian *hôtel* transformed into a medieval manor. The foyer was filled with the gem-like glow of Willette's stained glass bay

[1] Général Boulanger, 'hero on horseback', possibly the most popular, certainly the most colourful of *la belle époque*'s political figures, might with his wide-spread support have engineered a seizure of power and a return to royalist government. However, passion for his mistress, Madame de Bonnemain, led him to follow her out of France after she had been forcefully persuaded to leave by cunning government republicans. When Madame de Bonnemain died a year later, Général Boulanger stabbed himself to death on her grave. The complex yet farcical story of this hero who had given up an entire nation for passion, was worthy of several wags of the Chat Noir's satirical tail.

20

AU THÉATRE-LIBRE

window, representing in Symbolist fashion the story of the golden calf. Near the door was a printed evocation to all: 'Passer-by, stop . . . This edifice has been consecrated to the Muses and to joy under the auspices of the Chat Noir. Passer-by, be modern!' Each of the floors, including Salis's personal Salle de Conseil, was decorated with a profligacy of paintings and sketches by the modern masters of Montmartre, medieval armour, Japanese masks and *objets trouvés* of all kinds.

Salis presided as host and conférencier, a participatory master of ceremonies or compère. He would welcome his guests in his absurdly formal academician's style and invite them to his first floor Salle des Poètes-chansonniers. Here Maurice Donnay, later a member of the Académie Française, might be reciting aphoristic verse; or Jules Jouy might be chanting a critique of Boulanger while the General sat on the premises:

AU CHAT-NOIR

> *Ouvriers et rustres*
> *Assez de pasteurs!*
> *Plus de chefs illustres!*
> *De triomphateurs!*
> *La levée en masse*
> *Forge des héros.*
> *En France, on se passe*
> *Bien des généraux!*
>
> Workers and peasants,
> We've had enough of priests,
> Conquering heroes
> And illustrious chiefs.
> A mass insurrection
> Forges its own heroes.
> France can well do without
> Any more generals.

But the true centre of the new Chat Noir was the Théâtre d'Ombres, the shadow theatre, a brain child of Henri Rivière which put all the Paris *beau monde* into a state of wonder by the brilliance of its technical and artistic innovation. The Théâtre d'Ombres was a discovery in the true cabaret spirit. It was a genre which could be used for a variety of effects and incorporated all genres into a small scale replica of Wagner's 'total art work' (*Gesamtkunstwerk*).

Using an ingenious combination of shadow and light play, decor painted or superimposed on glass and paper, cut-outs and Japanese-style puppets, Rivière created unparalleled pre-cinematographic effects on the screen-stage. These were underlined by musical accompaniment, with a choir of sometimes up to twenty people backstage, piano or organ; by narration, either of the story-telling or satirical commentary kind; and by acting. The diversity of the shadow plays does credit to the eclectic black cat. One could pass without transition from the mysticism of Georges Fragerolle's *L'Enfant prodigue*, to

AU MOULIN-ROUGE

21

Caran d'Ache, view of the interior of the Chat Noir during a shadow play, 1887. Musée du vieux Montmartre.

Maurice Donnay's Athenian drama, *Phryné*, to the parodied naturalism of Louis Morin's, *Pierrot pornographe*, to the heroic epic, *Epopée*, which put Paris once again into a Napoleonic mood of patriotic jubilation. *Epopée*, a military play in two acts and fifty tableaux, was created by Caran d'Ache, one of the epoch's leading poster artists. Witnesses say that some of the shadow plays equalled in beauty Turner's impressionistic effects.

One kind of shadow play consisted of a satirical montage of current events, *pièce bonimontée*, a newsreel with a difference. Salis, known by then as the Seigneur de Chatonville-en-Vexin, would improvise a commentary, drawing in references to any notables in the audience. He had respect for nothing and no one, and with an insolent loquacity, Salis would allow his sharp sense of the actual to demolish bankers and the treasury, politicians and parliamentarianism, 'the *grand monde*, the *demi-monde*, *tout le monde* . . .' In this room, with its profligacy of cats in diverse positions and styles, Salis cast the mould for what was to become the cabaret tradition of the conférencier.

Salis had the talent of a great impressario. In the later days of the cabaret Salis's verbal improvisations were accompanied by piano

22

One of the original cut-outs for the shadow play *L'Epopée* by Caran d' Ache. Musée du vieux Montmarte.

Clairs de Lune, an impressionist shadow play by Henri Rivière with music and poetry by Georges Fragerolle, 1897. Musée du vieux Montmartre.

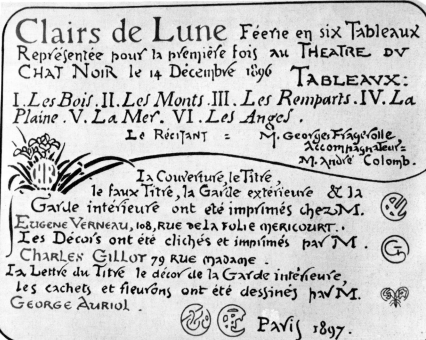

One of the images in the shadow play *Paris* by Henri Callot. Musée du vieux Montmartre.

23

LE "CHAT NOIR" SE BALLADE

improvisations from Erik Satie. Because of a quarrel with Salis, the twenty-two year old Satie – Esoterik Satie as Alphonse Allais dubbed him – only stayed at the Chat Noir for a few months and went on to become pianist at the Auberge du Clou where he made friends with Claude Debussy. But it is to Salis's credit that he recognized the satirical genius of the avant-garde composer. Salis believed in encouraging new talent, and every night after the Théâtre d'Ombres had shut its doors, a small and varying group would meet in a back room of the Chat Noir. Here unknown composers, poets and chansonniers would perform for each other and practice their art. The cabaret had begun to function as an artistic laboratory, a revitalizing ground for tired artistic formulas. This role was to remain a highly significant one.

Before leaving the Chat Noir and the sound of that laughter which Rabelais called 'le propre de l'homme', one more figure must be met: Alphonse Allais, chief raconteur of la belle époque and recently acclaimed member of the universal 'Pataphysique Society' fathered by Alfred Jarry. For several years editor of the Chat Noir magazine, Allais was a monologuist, sketch-writer, and story-teller. His humour kept all Paris, high and low, waiting breathlessly for the paper which would carry his next tale. Allais was a consummate absurdist. From an ordinary phenomenon, simple sentiment or situation, he would logically deduce the looniest, most macabre, and most unexpected of results.

24

An example of Allais's method is a tale of a certain American, Dr Snowdrop, from his *Oeuvres anthumes* (so he names his pre-humous collection). This relates how the fictitious doctor, having remained celibate for fifty-five years, falls in love while doing his Christmas shopping with a very beautiful, very young, shop girl. He asks her to marry him on the spot, and on their wedding night, in the midst of a tender caress, tells her that, if she were ever to be unfaithful, she should contrive to keep him in ignorance of it, for her own benefit. The young wife quickly proceeds to fall in love with Dr Snowdrop's young medical protégé, and her husband intercepts one of her amorous notes passionately proclaiming her desire always to be with her lover, to blend their two beings into one. The doctor only murmurs, 'That's quite easy . . .' During that evening's dinner, he puts an anaesthetic into their food. The lovers fall asleep and the doctor performs a miraculous operation which simply consists of removing the respective left and right limbs of the couple and sewing their two bodies together. When the lovers awake, quite fit, but horrified at their tangible union, the American doctor only quotes his wife's letter and adds, 'This is what the French call a collage.'

The rigorous logic of this burlesque, as macabre as the black cat could wish it, was Allais's particular trademark.

Alphonse Allais as seen by Cabriol. The armband reads 'Practical Joking'. *L'Hydropathe*, 1880. Musée du vieux Montmartre.

Aristide Bruant by Toulouse-Lautrec.

Aristide Bruant and Le Mirliton

The Chat Noir's success made Montmartre the artistic centre of Paris and when the cabaret closed its doors in 1897, Salis could quite blatantly claim this achievement as a personal feat. *Chatnoiresque* became a current adjective of the period and entered the argot dictionary to describe all events which blended fantasy and humour with a degree of impudence. Numerous other cabarets sprang up around this original one: Cabaret des Quat'z' Arts, La Lune Rousse, Les Pantins, to mention only a few. But the most notable of these set up its headquarters in the old home of the Chat Noir and was called Le Mirliton, the reed pipe, which in French has the additional meaning of doggerel. Its particular genius can only be attributed to its originator, a swashbuckling chansonnier called Aristide Bruant whose remarkable presence has come down to us in Toulouse-Lautrec's posters. Discovered by Jules Jouy and trained in the school of the first of balladeers, François Villon, Bruant brought street poetry and the socio-critical song which are fundamental to the cabaret repertoire, to their contemporary zenith.

Bruant was the son of impoverished landowners, and was sent to Paris at the age of fifteen to earn his keep. These were the days when, as Bruant himself tells us, a lawyer's clerk earned only seventy-five francs a month, a worker from thirty-five to forty francs a week, and a railroad employee three francs twenty-five centimes a day, and the young Aristide had to make do with the cheapest possible bistros. A timid country boy, he was at first shocked by the language used in these most undignified surroundings, but little by little, he came to notice its original flavour, its humorous images which occasionally had the power of poetry. The street argot was colourful, lively, brutal, cynical, and rich in picturesque metaphor, daring neologisms and imitative harmony. He set out to learn it, taking as his masters those perambulatory professors he met on his long nightly walks in

The Cabaret La Lune Rousse. Bibliothèque historique de la ville de Paris.

26

the 'damned' city – vagabonds, prostitutes, ruffians, the dispossessed. Bruant not only educated himself in argot, but in the lives of the people who spoke it. Soon he was to recreate both in his songs making the art of the chansonnier what has been called the most human of all arts.

During military service Bruant composed songs for his mates, and once back in Paris, though working for the railway, he began to sing and recite in the smaller *cafés-concerts*. He was noticed by Jules Jouy, who brought him to the Chat Noir gatherings. Bruant became a familiar sight on the Butte Montmartre, and, as the years went by, something of a landmark. With his stature, his flamboyant black velvet jacket, red shirt, yellow waistband, scarf and high boots, he was both man of the people and artist.

In 1885 Bruant opened his own cabaret, decorating it with a variety of *bibelots*, a profusion of paintings by Steinlen, Toulouse Lautrec and others. While Salis's Chat Noir had maintained the 'bon ton' of the Academy it was spoofing, Bruant created an atmosphere which was the epitome of low life. Guests – *beau monde*, artists, populace – were greeted with a variety of slang expletives. (It is not coincidental that Bruant wrote his own dictionary of argot.) If a woman wandered in in the midst of a song, the audience were asked to join into a chorus of '*Oh là là, c'tte gueul' qu'elle a*', roughly translatable as 'Dig that kisser . . .' Bruant's was the initial theatre of provocation and audience insult. And the guests loved it. They had after all come for an evening of gutterization. Bruant claimed that he took his revenge for his past difficulties by treating his better guests 'like dung'. 'They laugh because they think I'm joking.' But, as he went on to claim, he was not merely joking.

Stomping back and forth on the wooden floor, Bruant would suddenly sit down, pick up his guitar, and yell out: 'Shut your row, blast you all, I'm going to sing.' And pacing again, he would sing, or rather, cry out in a voice at once abrasive and persuasive.

> J'suis républicain socialisse,
> Compagnon radical ultra
> Révolutionnaire, anarchisse,
> etc etc . . .
>
> C'est vrai que j'comprends pas grand' chose
> A tout c'qu'y dis'nt les orateurs,
> Mais j'sais qu'i's parl'nt pour la bonne cause
> Et qu'i's tap' a su' les exploiteurs.
>
> I am a republican socialist,
> An ultra radical comrade
> A revolutionary and an anarchist,
> etc. etc.
>
> It's true that I don't understand much
> Of what the orators say,
> But I know they're speaking for the good old cause
> And they sure knock the exploiters okay.

Poster for *La Vache Enragée* (Cabaret and Magazine) by Roedel 1897. 'The enraged cow' was also the name given to the principal float in the 'Fête de la Vachalade', a yearly Montmartre festival organized by the Chat Noir group. Its purpose, the chroniclers say, was to remind the Montmartre inhabitants that they 'didn't give a damn' about their poverty. Bibliothèque historique de la ville de Paris.

27

In this song, entitled 'No More Bosses', as in many of his others, Bruant takes on the voice of the exploited innocent. Should a guest happen to leave in the midst of one of his numbers, Bruant would stop and the audience would join him in the refrain:

Tous les clients sont des cochons
La faridon don don, la far dondaine,
Et surtout les ceuss qui s'en vont,
La faridondain' la fari don don.

All customers are swine,
Especially those who go before time.

Bruant's best songs are evocations of street life, grimly placed in their milieu. He pleaded the cause of those condemned by birth to abject misery and exposed the despair of those victims of social injustice who live without fire, home, or bread. With a mordant melancholy, he sang of prisoners and prostitutes, of the outcasts spawned by a city which refused to recognize them.

A's sont des tas	They are those
Qu'ont pus d'appas	With no more charm
Et qui n'ont pas	Not a penny
L'sou dans leur bas.	In their hose.
Pierreuses,	Street-walkers,
Trotteuses,	Sidewalk-stompers,
A's marchent l'soir,	They walk at night,
Quand il fait noir,	When there's no more light,
Sur le trottoir.	On the sidewalks.
Les ch'veux frisés,	Hair frizzé
Les seins blasés,	Breasts blasés,
Les seins blasés,	Breasts blasés,
Les pieds usés	Feet worn away.
Christ aux yeux doux,	Christ with mild eyes,
Qu'es mort pour nous,	Who died for our lives,
Chauff' la terre oùs-	Warm the earth where
qu'on fait leurs trous.	Holes are dug for them.

The people listened, even those upon whose heads Bruant hurled his insults.

Bruant once remarked that he regretted the passing of those days in the military when he didn't have to yell himself hoarse from ten in the evening until two in the morning in order to entertain a band of 'idiots' who not only did not understand what he was singing, but who also could not understand what hunger meant — 'those who were born with silver spoons in their mouths'. The statement is typical of Bruant's bitterness, yet it does not take account of the profound belief in the possibility of social change which his songs constantly echo. As one listens to the songs of *Dans la rue*, those songs which

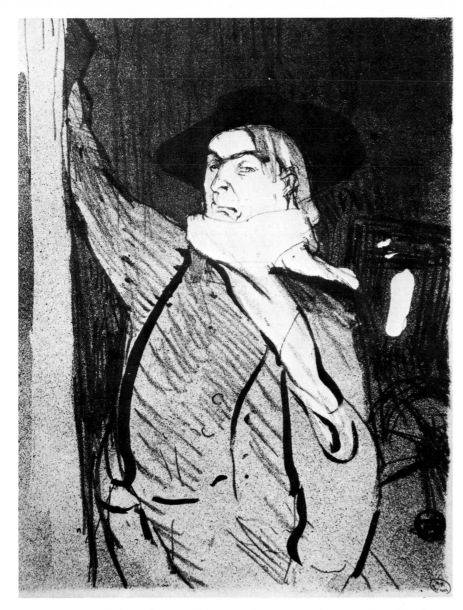

Aristide Bruant. Litho by Toulouse-Lautrec. Bibliothèque historique de la ville de Paris.

evoke the daily life of every Parisian district in the way that Toulouse Lautrec's art does, Bruant emerges as a self-conscious social critic. Society can save its outcasts if only it can be made to see their plight and its responsibility. And with a deep affinity for the subjects of his songs, without a trace of moralistic sentimentality, Bruant does make one see.

In 1898 Bruant was nominated by his Parisian 'home' district, Belleville, to stand as a candidate for the legislature. The song he wrote for his election campaign illuminates the motivating force behind his choice of the art of the chanson, as well as his deeply human politics.

> Si j'étais votre deputé,
> Ohe! Ohe! qu'on se le dise –
> J'ajouterais Humanité
> Aux trois mots de notre devise.
> Au lieu de parler tous les jours
> Pour la république ou l'empire –
> Et de faire de longs discours,
> Pour ne rien dire.

29

Yvette Guilbert by Toulouse-Lautrec, 1893. Bibliothèque historique de la ville de Paris.

*Je parlerais des petits fieux
Des filles-mère, des pauvres vieux
Qui l'hiver, gêlent par la ville,
Ils auraient chaud, comme en été
Si j'étais nommé deputé
A Belleville.*

If I were your deputy,
Oho! Oho! one can only try –
I would add the word Humanity
To the three of our revolutionary cry.
Instead of speaking every day
For the republic or the empire –
And making lengthy speeches,
Which have nothing to say

I'd speak of the small sons
Of unwed mothers, of the poor old people
Who in winter, freeze throughout the city,
They would be as warm as in summer
If I were made deputy
In Belleville.

Bruant's songs penetrated beyond the walls of the Mirliton to become the basis of the cabaret chanson tradition. In particular, they were taken up by Yvette Guilbert, one of the few women who performed 'cabaretistically' at that time. Yvette Guilbert had developed her style in the *cafés-concerts* and with them she grew into music hall. Long and thin, with sharp angular gestures and bright, reddish hair, her presence and delivery were a set of contradictions which enticed her audiences. She was at once the weary, ageing, cynical coquette, and the pure English governess longing for a spiritual love. Her hoarse, mournful voice with its touch of hysteria could both bring to life Bruant's harlots and infuse meaning into a sentimental lyric. Guilbert was an actress in song, an authentic *diseuse* who 'spoke, sang, prophesied' her numbers, and her mode was to be recreated in cabarets for the next half century. Yet despite her link with the early cabaret tradition, she did not actually perform in the noted cabarets. Her stage was the Divan Japonais, the Moulin Rouge, Les Ambassadeurs, headquarters of variety spectacle and later concert halls and universities around the world. As for cabaret, the form had to travel to Germany before women became an integral part of its make-up.

30

Cabaret Travels East: Freedom is Tingeltangel 1900–1914

Berlin

Wilhelmine Germany provided a far less free-spirited environment than Paris. The hierarchical authority structure, with its multifarious uniformed officials, encouraged 'yes-men' and political disaffection rather than critical attitudes directed towards change. Corruption was rife; religion a mere lip-service. And while a sombre sense of duty to family, business and state was the prized attribute of the German burgher, it only thinly veiled that desire for material gain which constituted success. *Kultur* was something one recognized and respected when its high tone induced a state of incomprehending awe akin to boredom. Yet as Golo Mann tells us, 'The Wilhelmine style was devoid of taste, with its court poets, court painters, and court preachers, its speeches in honour of the Kaiser's birthday and its Sedan celebrations, with its ostentatious buildings, barracks and mock castles.' Censorship, especially where the dramatic arts were concerned, was strict, and rigid sexual morality prevailed. If certain kinds of literature and art flourished – and the period was rich in this – they were not initially those which levelled an overtly satirical gaze at the state of society and German culture. By 1900, however, the tide was turning. The influence of Nietzsche and his tireless and biting criticism of philistinism had begun to spread to a variety of quarters. Humour and the Dionysian elements could be properly regarded as part of art. Young artists and intellectuals, rebelling against the moral and social norms and standards of taste of the bourgeoisie and court circles, turned to them.

A number of near-simultaneous factors then contributed to the birth of German cabaret. Of primary importance was the gossip from France concerning the vital bohemian ambiance of Montmartre and the creation there of a new artistic form, the cabaret. Albert Langen, who had spent some time in Paris came back to Munich imbued with the satirical spirit of the Chat Noir and *Gil Blas Illustré*. With a group of others, including Frank Wedekind who had similarly imbibed the Montmartre air, he launched the illustrated satirical weekly, *Simplicissimus*. Destined to keep all of Germany, high and low, on its toes for several decades, *Simplicissimus* attacked the makers, purveyors and accepters of authority, literary kitsch and hypocritical morality. Its spirit made it the kin of cabaret.

Then, in 1900, Otto Julius Bierbaum, the poet, impressed by the mode of the French sung lyric and seeing its potential for 'bringing

Th. Th. Heine's view of Bierbaum (standing), Wozogen, and a chansonnier. From *Simplicissimus*.

31

'The Power of the Uniform' by Olaf
Gulbransson in *Simplicissimus*, 1906.

art to the people', published a collection of singable poems entitled,
Deutsche Chansons. The book included native German poetry which
could lend itself to song, including Richard Dehmel, Arno Holz,
Detlev von Liliencron, Ernst von Wolzogen and Wedekind. In his
epistolary preface to the collection, Bierbaum points out that his
aim was to make art pervade the entirety of life. Painters today, he
says, are making chairs for people to sit on, not for museums. Just so
poets now wish to write poems that can not only be read in quiet
chambers, but performed in front of a joyous mass. 'Applied lyric –
that is our battle cry!' Within a year *Deutsche Chansons* had sold
20,000 copies and many editions were to follow.

It is worth noting that the perennial German tendency to look on
culture as an orthopedic appliance is evident in Bierbaum's rallying
cry. A plastic medium, the cabaret would in Germany lose some of the
playful tone of its French originators and take on the more serious
and more satirically aggressive impetus of its German makers.

Bierbaum's intent of functionalizing and revolutionizing poetry can
be seen as a part of the *Jugendstil* movement. His specific desire to
'ennoble', to raise to the level of serious art the *Tingeltangel* or
popular variety show, locates another starting-point for the German
cabaret. Modern city man, Bierbaum says, has *Varieténerven*, variety
nerves. He wants change. And Bierbaum was prepared to elevate the
ordinary man's taste by giving him variety on an artistic level.
'Freedom is tingeltangel', the saying went, linking artistic freedom
with the German name for variety spectacle. The adoption of popular
forms, for whatever motive cultural or political, was to remain a part
of the cabaret tradition throughout.

After the appearance of *Deutsche Chansons*, things moved quickly.
Ernst von Wolzogen, aristocrat and poet, opened the Überbrettl' in
Berlin. *Brettl'* is the term for the popular stage and Wolzogen added
the *über*, thinking of Nietzsche's *Übermensch*, to designate his desire
for a performance medium which used the elements of the variety
show and transcended or ennobled these. He rented a theatre of 650
seats, and with himself as conférencier set out to establish a programme which would contain that magical mixture of satire, eroticism
and lyricism which the French cabaret had originated.

The opening night of the Überbrettl' in Berlin presented in its
first half a part of Arthur Schnitzler's *Anatol* cycle, a pantomime

N⁰ᵉ Série — 9ᵉ Année — N° 113   Prix : 10 centimes   9 Juin 1893

Le Mirliton

Hebdomadaire, paraît le Vendredi

Prix de l'Abonnement

	France	Étranger
Un an	6 fr.	10 fr.
Six mois	4 fr.	6 fr.
Trois mois	3 fr.	4 fr.

DIRECTEUR

ARISTIDE BRUANT

84, Boulevard Rochechouart

Adresser tout ce qui concerne
la Rédaction et l'Administration
à M. FABRICE LÉMON
Secrétaire de la Rédaction

7, rue d'Enghien, Paris

Les quat'patt's c'est les chiens d'Paris,
Les voyous, les clebs ed'barrière,
C'est les ceux qui sont jamais pris...
Qui va jamais à la fourrière.

. . . .
. . . .

Car c'est pas des toutous d'Agnès
Ni des cabots d'propriétaires ;
C'est mêm' pas des chiens d'locataires,
I's sont lib's comm' Mossieu Barrès.

Voir la suite au verso.

Pierrot play, a shadow play by Liliencron, a subtle lyricist, plus a mixture of poems and chansons performed by women as well as men. The second half began with a parody of d'Annunzio written by Christian Morgenstern, whose gallows ballads and linguistically innovative 'nonsense' verses were seminal avant-garde German poetry. It was followed by the hit of the evening and indeed of Berlin for the next few months, Bierbaum's operetta-play *Der lustige Ehemann* (*The Merry Husband*) set to the music of the house composer, Oscar Straus. In Biedermeir costume, the happy married couple sang, bubbled, bobbed, danced:

> *Ringelringelrosenkranz*
> I dance with my wife
> We dance around the rose bush
> *Klingklanggloribusch*
> I dance round peacock-like.

Wolzogen's Überbrettl' was not really a cabaret. The scale of the theatre did not permit that essential cabaret intimacy to exist, nor did his programmes – partially due to censorship – have the satirical bite of the best cabarets. As conférencier Wolzogen played the witty court fool who was permitted to speak truths, but never the acid wit who could stir his audience beyond laughter by insult. The Überbrettl' did, however, achieve the ennobling of the variety show which it had set out to attain and it made the chanson form part of the German repertory. Around the Überbrettl', a number of small cabaret-like ventures sprang up, as well as large-scale competition.

In 1901, Max Reinhardt, then a young actor and unknown as a director, together with a group of young intellectuals and artists conducted a benefit performance for Morgenstern, who needed support in order to be sent to a sanatorium. The performance consisted of parodies: of Schiller's *Don Carlos* done as a naturalist drama *à la* Hauptmann and entitled, *Karle, A Thief's Comedy*; as a symbolic-mystical play *à la* Maeterlinck, *Carleas and Elisande*; and as a take-off by strolling players. The one-act parodies were interspersed with satirical commentaries on monarchy, songs and poems. The evening was a roaring success and the group decided to stay together and do weekly performances.

A name had to be found and they had none. Goethe came to their aid: '*Name ist Schall und Rauch*' and Schall und Rauch, sound and smoke, it was to be. The group rented a space, created a stage in the form of a Greek temple and performed their parodies. It is interesting to note that Berlin had a large enough knowledgeable theatre public at that time to permit an on-going response to literary parody. The police, implementers of state censorship, were however not quite so enlightened, and when Morgenstern did a parody of a Hohenzollern poet, they interceded. Reinhardt's group was to suffer from the strict censorship many times.

The Schall und Rauch after several months, metamorphosed into the Kleine Theatre, one of Germany's first experimental theatres. Rein-

34

hardt was not really a cabaret man, although his liking for the form was evident in the related 'revue' quality of much of his later directing. In the meantime, however, the group had worked out one further direction for the German cabaret: cabaret as a vehicle for satirizing other literature. These literary origins marked the tradition.

The cabaret had also begun its Berlin existence in its role as meeting place and locale for performance. Max Tilke's *Der Hungrige Pegasus* (The Hungry Pegasus), with its caricatures on walls and bistro atmosphere, was a direct copy of the French cabaret. Here, one night a week, poets, writers and painters would gather, smoke, talk, and perform samples of their work. Peter Hille, street vagabond and impressionist poet, recited here. Elsa Laura Seeman sang to the music of her lute, and the writer Hans Hyan, audience-insulter in good Bruant fashion, performed. The strictures of Wilhelmine Germany and the courage of these early cabaretists becomes evident when one realizes that as apolitical a lyric poet as Hille – who was to die several years later alone on a street bench – was constantly an object of suspicion for the police. Hans Hyan's chansons on the unemployed, on adverse social conditions and the fate of the poor, then seem truly remarkable. This first German socialist rebel in song, who opened his own cabaret, would take on the voice of the dispossessed and yell out: 'Damm you all./We want to know/Why you're all full/ And we have to go hungry.'

Munich

Germany's artistic centre at the turn of the century was Munich. Here in the Schwabing district, which picturesquely surrounds the English Gardens, writers, musicians, painters, eccentrics, faddists of innumerable persuasions, and intellectuals congregated in the many cafés. At one and the same time this bohemian quarter, which echoed the tone of Montmartre, played host to a variety of émigrés including both Thomas Mann and Lenin (variously known as Herr Meyer and Dr Jourdanoff), a figure who mysteriously shadows the cabaret's various locales but is never actively involved in its doings. By 1900 Munich's bustling avant-garde had rebelled against old forms and created its own Secessionist movement. The Art Nouveau magazine, *Jugend*, was in full flower, and the satirical weekly, *Simplicissimus*, found its home here. Munich was in the grips of an artistic renaissance despite – or perhaps because of – the numerous, but well-defined, restrictions which Wilhelmine law imposed.

And Munich had its Fasching, that pre-lenten carnival which momentarily gathers all the populace into the undifferentiated exuberance of celebration. For one brief part of the year, all sectors of Munich society are reconciled in the spirit of carnival laughter. Ingenious masquerades and pranks, processions of grotesquely colourful floats, a throwing off of sexual inhibitions, music, mime, street

35

IVGEND 1903 № 8

Jul. Diez

Yvette Guilbert in a poster by Bac. Bibliothèque historique de la ville de Paris.

The Jugendstil revolution in the decorative arts. Cover of the *Jugend* magazine, 1903.

acting, characterize this moment of creative extravagance. Presiding over it all is the spirit of the clown who anarchically cocks a snook at everything in the world, mocks its inanities and includes himself in the resulting laughter. It is in the carnival, with its air of popular festivity, its gay and simultaneously mocking laughter, its variety of spectacles in which witnesses and performers are one, that we find the age-old ancestor of the cabaret.

In his book *Rabelais and his World*, Mikhail Bakhtin notes that the carnival spirit consecrates inventive freedom; liberates man from the prevailing viewpoint of the world, its conventions, established truths and humdrum clichés; and offers him a new outlook on reality. This too is the essence of cabaret, though the form, self-consciously created by individual men, did not always attain to the fullness of this potential.

It is possibly the coincidence of creative talent with the native experience of carnival which resulted in Munich's producing one of the most fertile and interesting of European cabarets, and in the course of time, an exceptional comedian-clown who was to influence Brecht, Karl Valentin.

Munich's bohemia gathers for a Simplicissimus party, 1909. Theater-Museum, Munich.

The masks of the Eleven Executioners, designed by Wilheim Hüsgen. Klaus Budzinski Archiv.

The Eleven Executioners

Members of the Munich bohemia were adamant about the strictly imposed morality law, the Lex Heinze, which permitted police interference in art. This could take the form of censorship, confiscation of an edition of a book or an issue of a magazine, deletion of one part of a performance, or, more radically, imprisonment of the offending artist or publicist. Banding together to fight this law, artists, painters and students formed the Goethe Alliance for the Protection of Free Art and Science. During the carnival of 1901 members of this group, including the *Simplicissimus* editor Langen, and Wedekind, paraded through the streets in masquerade, carrying protest placards and singing their battle hymn. It claimed that they were prepared to do anything against the Lex Heinze except 'streak'.

The group was composed of young Secessionist painters, *Simplicissimus* staff and contributors, and students and actors from the Academic Dramatic Union, among whom was the director Otto Falkenberg. Following directly from this Fasching protest, eleven members of the group decided to form a cabaret which would continue their battle against archaic morality and the conventions of the establishment. Taking their cue from the legal system they were attacking, they called themselves *Die Elf Scharfrichter*, the eleven executioners. What they were to execute was social hypocrisy itself.

Having raised money from a variety of quarters, they rented a small theatre, and decorated it with grotesque masks of the eleven and drawings by their contemporaries from *Jugend* and *Simplicissimus*, Felicien Rops and Steinlen. The tables and chairs seating a hundred were comfortable enough, but a grim tone was set by torture and execution implements the group had gathered. As their emblem, they chose a skull wearing a judge's wig and a pillory. The theatre had a sunken orchestra pit, rare in those days, and a modern lighting system which had been installed for special effects. Technically it was at the peak of its time. The stage was set for Munich's first cabaret.

These hangmen of the status quo knew that if they performed publicly they would be harassed by censorship, and so they called themselves a 'club' which played only to 'invited guests', one night a week.

39

täglich
Die 11
Scharfrichter
Türkenstr. 28

Marya Delvard. Eleven Executioners poster by Th. Th. Heine. Theater-Museum, Munich.

Every programme, however, stated quite openly how one could obtain an invitation. The Executioners chose blood-curdling names for themselves: Marc Henry, a French journalist stationed in Munich, who had had some experience as chansonnier and conférencier at the Chat Noir, called himself Balthasar Starr, or corpse-rigid. Leo Kreiner, critic and lyricist, became Dionysius Tod (Death); Otto Falkenberg, one of the main initiators of the group, Peter Luft (Wind); Richard Weinhöppel, the talented composer, Hannes Ruch. Others were

Opposite
The Dance of the Eleven Executioners. Theater-Museum Munich.

41

Interior of The Eleven Executioners.
Theater-Museum Munich.

Till Blut, Frigidius Strang, Max Knax, Serapion Grab, Kaspar Beil, Gottfried Still, and Willibaldus Rost. The sounds speak for themselves.

Friday, 13 April 1901. Opening night. Marc Henry, alias Balthasar Starr, standing on a high step overlooking the orchestra pit, welcomes some of his illustrious guests by name. Then Hannes Ruch's music strikes the chords of the eleven executioners' theme song. Dressed in blood-red gowns with slit-eyed cowls and yielding executioners' hatchets, they dance on stage, hands joined, and sing in *basso profundo*.

> It looms on high that black block
> We judge heartily but pierce.
> Blood red heart, blood red frock,
> Our fun is always fierce.
> Any enemy of the time
> Will bloodily executed be.
> Whoever is a friend of death,
> Adorn with song and sound will we.

This theme song was followed by chansons and recitation by both male and female members of the group and its wider entourage known as the *Henkersknechte* or hangman's apprentices. Then came *The Veterinary Surgeon*, a parody by Hanns von Gumppenberg of Maeterlinck's mysticism. This was followed by a biting satire on Germany's growing imperialistic pretensions, done as a giant puppet play and called *The Good Family*. Wilhelm II, with his unrealistic political aspirations and his statement that Germany's future lay 'on the water', that is, in building up a sea power equal to Britain's, was an object of constant criticism to the Executioners and their fellows. After its first performance, *The Good Family* was censored out of the programme by the authorities.

Up to this point the audience had been appreciative but not inordinately enthusiastic. Then enter Marya Delvard, first stage vamp of the century. Thin, tall, pale, red-haired, wide-mouthed, wearing the expression of a grand tragedienne, and clad in a simple, high-necked, clinging black dress, she intoned with tired melancholy the words of Wedekind's *Ilse*.

> *Ich war ein Kind von fünfzehn Jahren,*
> *Ein reines, unschuldsvolles Kind,*
> *Als ich zum erstenmal erfahren,*
> *Wie süss der Liebe Freuden sind.*
>
> *Er nahm mich um den Leib und lachte*
> *Und flüsterte: O, welch ein Glück!*
> *Und dabei bog er sachte, sachte*
> *Den Kopf mir auf das Pfühl zurück.*
>
> *Seit jenem Tag lieb' ich sie alle,*
> *Des Lebens schönster Lenz ist mein.*
> *Und wenn ich keinem mehr gefalle,*
> *Dann will ich gern begraben sein.*

I was a child of fifteen,
A pure, innocent child,
When I first experienced,
How sweet the joys of love are.

He hugged me round and laughed
And whispered: Oh what joy!
And then he bent my head gently, gently
Down onto the pillow.

Since that day I love them all,
Life's most beautiful spring is mine.
And when I no longer please anyone,
I will gladly be buried.

Marya Delvard. Klaus Budzinski Archiv.

An electric thrill went through the audience. The Eleven Executioners were a total success.

Marya Delvard, the daughter of a Parisian professor, had been educated in a convent in Lothringen. She came to Munich in order to study music and there met her countryman, Marc Henry. The two-some formed a memorable cabaret team which travelled throughout Europe. Henry, the only professional in the original Executioners' group was well aware that for a cabaret to be successful it must have a variety of acts and the relationship between audience and performers must remain a very relaxed and intimate one. The stage or platform is something anyone can perform on if he or she so wishes, and the acts themselves must maintain an immediacy and an improvisatory aspect. But even Marc Henry could not have been prepared for the improvisatory nature of Marya Delvard's performance on that opening night.

In the excitement and bustle of that evening, Otto Falkenberg reminisces, Delvard's première dress had been ripped from top to bottom. The hurry was great and it could not be fixed, so she had to perform in her ordinary day dress, which in the style of the time was rather tight. Marc Henry pulled it a little tighter and had violet light play over it while she was on stage in order to hide its true nature. The dress accentuated Marya's pallor, had a shock effect somewhat akin to jeans being worn for the first time by a woman on stage, and became her trademark. Indeed, in Ernst Stern's caricature silhouette it emerged as one of the emblems of the Executioners.

Among the many talents which the Executioners possessed, one which towered over all the others was Frank Wedekind. Wedekind joined the group several months after its initiation, and since Willy Rath had dropped out, became one of its core members. Feeling that his name had a sufficiently 'frightening' effect on a public to which he was already notorious, Wedekind did not take on a pseudonym like the other Executioners. A radically innovative dramatist and poet, Wedekind was seen by his friends as a mixture of anarchist and saint. His chilling portrayal of man's instinctual drives, his frank evocation of sexuality, his denunciation of the hypocrisy of prevailing moral codes – all were intended to shock the bourgeoisie out of its dull

43

Frank Wedekind as seen by B. F. Dolbin in *Jugend*.

complacency, and did not exactly endear Wedekind to the censors. Indeed, little of his work could be performed at this time without creating a scandal.

Wedekind's battle with authority was one of long standing. In 1898 under the pseudonym Hieronymous he had published a ballad in *Simplicissimus* entitled 'Palästinafahrt', which satirically spoofed the Kaiser's trip to the Holy Land. The ballad genially mocks the Kaiser's great love of costume, and his joy in being photographed. The result was a suit for lèse majesté. The Kaiser was insulted and the anonymous offender had to be found. Wedekind believed that his original manuscript had been done away with after printing, but unfortunately this was not the case, and the writing was identified as his. However, with a wink of the eye from the Schwabing police chief in question, Wedekind was effectively told, 'We don't know you yet, but we will tomorrow . . .' He had time to perform in the première of *Earth Spirit* that night, drink with his friends afterwards, and then dash off to Paris where the *Simplicissimus* publisher, Langen, had already fled. Thomas Theodor Heine, who had created a caricature of the Kaiser to go along with the ballad, had been arrested and sentenced to six months. Hearing of Heine's fate, Wedekind returned to Germany and offered himself up to the law. He was similarly jailed for six months and spent the turn of the century behind bars.

When he began to perform at the Executioners, Wedekind was already a recognized 'revolutionary'. He had certainly not stopped writing his satirical songs, nor indeed publishing them in *Simplicissimus*. His stage presence is said to have been enormous and his effect, especially upon the female members of his audience, electric. He would walk casually onto the stage, look contemptuously at his audience, and in a raw, jarring, high-pitched, slightly nasal voice which sharply articulated each syllable and forced its content upon his listeners, he would sing to his own tune:

> *Ich hab meine Tante geschlachtet,*
> *Meine Tante war alt und schwach,*
> *Ich hatte bei ihr übernachtet*
> *Und grub in den Kisten-Kasten nach.*
>
> *Da fand ich goldene Haufen,*
> *Fand auch an Papieren gar viel,*
> *Und hörte die alte Tante schnaufen*
> *Ohne Mitleid und Zartgefühl.*
>
> *Was nutzt es, dass sie sich noch härme –*
> *Nacht war es rings um mich her –*
> *Ich stiess ihr den Dolch in die Därme,*
> *Die Tant schnaufte nicht mehr.*
>
> *Das Geld war schwer zu tragen,*
> *Viel schwerer die Tante noch.*
> *Ich fasste sie bebend am Kragen*
> *Und stiess sie ins tiefe Kellerloch.*

Ich hab meine Tante geschlachtet,
Meine Tante war alt und schwach,
Ihr aber, o Richter, ihr trachtet
Meiner blühenden Jugend – Jugend nach.

I have murdered dear Auntie Alice,
My Auntie so old and so frail.
Motivated by greed and malice
I went straight on the treasure trail.

Her little house was simply seething
With banknotes, with shares and with gold.
I heard my Auntie's heavy breathing
But that left me perfectly cold.

I just followed my intuition,
In the dark I opened her door
And knifed her without inhibition –
My Auntie sighed and breathed no more.

The golden coins were weighing me down,
Her body was heavy as lead,
But I dragged Auntie without a frown
Through the garden and into the shed.

I have murdered dear Auntie Alice,
My Auntie so old and so frail.
I'm young, so young, yet out of malice
They've sentenced me to life-long jail.

(translated by Dorethea Gotfurt)

Plastic, drastic, and above all diabolic, so the adjectives described Wedekind's balladeering run. His harshly ironic, satanic tone, brittle and abrasive, was one Brecht imitated and it became the mark of the German cabaret song style. In 1918 Brecht wrote an obituary for Wedekind in the *Augsburger Neueste Nachrichten*, in which he made his admiration for the man and the dramatist clear, and evoked his vital presence. 'His vitality was his finest characteristic. He had only to enter a lecture hall full of hundreds of noisy students, or a room, or a stage, with his special walk, his sharply-cut bronze skull slightly tilted and thrust forward, and there was silence . . . There he stood, ugly, brutal, dangerous, with close-cropped red hair, his hands in his trouser pockets, and one felt that the devil himself couldn't shift him . . . A few weeks ago at the Bonbonnière he sang his songs to a guitar accompaniment in a brittle voice, slightly monotonous and quite untrained. No singer ever gave me such a shock, such a thrill. It was the man's intense aliveness, the energy which allowed him to defy sniggering ridicule and proclaim his brazen hymn to humanity, that also gave him this personal magic.'

When Wedekind returned from his imprisonment, he composed a satirical allegory of his fate as an insulter of majesty. His persona is a zoologist from Berlin, the very nature of whose work – since it includes scientific observation of the animal world – makes him into an offender of majesty, according to the authorities. Having described the zoologist's trial and imprisonment for lèse majesté, the narrator draws a moral:

> Therefore guard against zoological studies
> Youth, while you are young,
> For there slumbers in all the beasts
> A lèse majesté.

Wedekind's gift for satire extended into parody, as the ballad he composed as a take-off of 'Deutschland, Deutschland über alles' evidences. It begins,

> Muzzle, muzzle over everything,
> When the muzzle is properly placed,
> Then one will in the worst of instances
> Still be used as a court poet.

This attack on censorship appeared under a pseudonym in one of the many issues of *Simplicissimus* to be confiscated.

One of the most important features of the Executioners cabaret was that it included within its programme avant-garde dramatic works, which might not have found a place in the established theatres of the time. Sets were often designed by the talented artists of *Simplicissimus* and *Jugend*. The first part of Wedekind's *Earth Spirit* was put on here, as well as the première of his *Kaiserin von Neufundland*. The story of the *Earth Spirit* production is a famous one in Wedekind annals. Wedekind wanted Lulu to be played by a naive, inexperienced, but of course sensual, girl. Falkenberg told him that this would be just about impossible, but Wedekind insisted that he would find one. He did. One day a Lulu-like girl appeared on the Executioners' stage. Very Lulu-like. But she could not act, and Wedekind finally had to agree to have her replaced. He was however enraged by the choice of Yella Wagner for the role. This highly intelligent actress did not conform to his image of a Lulu played by an unthinking woman. Despite all this, the *Earth Spirit* production was a success.

The Executioners also put on parody plays. One of these, entitled *The Neighbour* by Hanns von Gumppenberg, deserves attention in theatre history, for it was a telling premonition of what Futurist performance was to be like. Its intent was satirical and the butt of the satire was the naturalist dramatist Hauptmann, whose characters generally come to a crushing end. But the violence of action, the blunt following through of logic to its absurd and irrational end, and the speed of the sketch, all foreshadowed later experimental forms.

The Neighbour is a 'monodrama in one sentence'. It has eight characters, only one of whom speaks, namely, the neighbour. A good civil servant, he enters the home of his neighbours, formally and politely. He apologizes for disturbing the seven, but he merely wishes to tell them of a few things he has observed over the last while. The

46

tempo of his sentence mounts as he publicly reveals to the family their own doings: adultery, internal fraud, incest. While he makes these revelations, they become increasingly agitated, fight with each other and finally die, are murdered, or commit suicide in a bizarre variety of ways. The neighbour politely wishes the corpses 'good night' and leaves as he came in.

Though the resonance of the Eleven Executioners was enormous, their actual life-span was not very long. By 1903, after touring to different parts of the country, the group had in essence disbanded. However, several of its members were instrumental in bringing cabaret to that eastern-most centre of pre-war Europe, Vienna.

Vienna: Nachtlicht and Fledermaus

In 1906 Marya Delvard and Marc Henry, together with the composer Richard Weinhöppel, opened the Nachtlicht, the night-light, on the Ballgasse in Vienna.

In these early years of the century Vienna was a resplendent cultural centre. From the avant-garde thrust of the Art Nouveau movement and the design-oriented Wiener Werkstätte to Adolphe Loos's architectural revolution in Functionalism, and to Mahler's symphonic extravagances, all aspects of the arts were flourishing. If this Imperial *caput mundi*, this gigantic head proliferating in intellectual and cultural brilliance, was somewhat dissociated from the dismembered parts of its vast bureaucratic body, the cataclysmic result had not yet been made brutally evident. Freud might be burrowing into the dark crevices of the Viennese mind, but on the surface that century-old characteristic of *gemütlichkeit* prevailed, a comfortable security shaped by a faith in the paternalist good-will of an apparently un-budgeable monarchy.

At the centre of Vienna's cultural life loomed the *Neue Freie Presse*, a bastion of the liberal press. It was said somewhat ironically of the *Neue Freie Presse* in those days that those who did not read it assiduously were abysmally out of touch with the pulse beat of contemporaneity. But those who did had all of the cultural mainstream at their fingertips and need not really read anything else. Every week half of the newspaper's front page was devoted to a bantering, impromptu, often impressionistic essay on any topic, or in fact several, known as the *Feuilleton*. Stephan Zweig notes that the appearance of the weekly feuilleton was as important a Viennese event as the opening of a new play or opera. He, like many of the Viennese literati, was a master of it.

Elegant, chatty, whimsical, the feuilleton was the emanation of the Viennese spirit of the time. It grew naturally out of the wit of café talk. And the numerous cafés of Vienna were the true homes of her artists, intellectuals, politicians and bohemians: meeting places where movements were concocted and ideas hatched. Just as the spoken feuilleton, and the witty narrative, marked Vienna's personal

Cabaret Fledermaus programme. Design by Moritz Jung. Osterreichisches Museum für angewandte Kunst.

Opposite
Cabaret Fledermaus programme, by Moritz Jung, 1907. Klaus Budzinski Archiv.

contribution to the cabaret, especially to the role of its conférencier, so the café inhabitants provided its ready-made audience and participants. From café to cabaret was a very small step. Even Karl Kraus, the satirical scourge of Vienna who, in a single-handedly written magazine, *Die Fackel* (Torch), waged a one-man war against the liberal press and its version of 'news', was a café frequenter and cabaret participant.

Vienna was in many ways a 'natural' city for cabaret. In the nineteenth century with dramatists and actors, Johann Nestroy and Ferdinand Raimund, it had its own national tradition of popular comic theatre. Indeed Nestroy, known as the Schopenhauer of the farce, was a master of the witty couplet, biting parody and topical satire. Not surprisingly, Kraus gave performance-readings of both these writers and brought them back into fashion. Then too, Vienna was the city of the operetta and of song. And finally, aphorism, verbal wit and topicality – the very ingredients of cabaret – were also the elements of Vienna's most popular written art form, the feuilleton.

48

Marc Henry and Marya Delvard at the Vienna cabaret Nachtlicht. Klaus Budzinski Archiv.

In all fairness, it must be noted that Kraus spilled some acerbic ink over the subject of the feuilleton. It was, he claimed, the apotheosis of *Schlamperei* in writing, that peculiarly Viennese mixture of carelessness and muddlement. Its breezy superficiality and subjectivism had infected the entire press and hastened the decline of the bourgeois world, which, he warned, would drown in a feuilletonistic sea of half-poetry and half-lies. But then, Kraus also defined a journalist as a man with no ideas and the ability to express them.

Nevertheless Kraus sang the praises of at least one feuilletoniste, Peter Altenberg, Vienna's most notorious drunk and arch bohemian. Altenberg, described by his friend Egon Friedell as 'a walking kaleidoscope of world views' wrote impressionistic vignettes of life in the modern metropolis. Mere fragments, these sketches are full of rootless individuals strolling from café to café. They capture the colour as well as the bohemian loneliness and tawdriness of Altenberg's own fragmentary life. Existence for the modern man, they suggest, consists of mere glimpses into the lives of others and bits of conversation overheard.

Like Altenberg, Kraus became a regular of the Nachtlicht. But Kraus's loyalties, always subject to quick quasi-paranoiac shifts,

50

suddenly turned. He wrote an article in *Die Fackel* criticizing the cabaret programme. The outcome was unusually violent. Erich Mühsam, then working at the Nachtlicht, reports in his memoirs that he was sitting in a wine bar with Kraus when Marc Henry and the Nachtlicht circle came in and sat down at another table. Suddenly Marc Henry charged over to their table and punched Kraus senseless. Mühsam himself, trying to make peace, was pushed aside, his knuckles bruised, and any further cabaret engagement broken. Meanwhile Peter Altenberg wandered amongst the disarranged tables muttering, 'I'm in despair', and drinking the remains of wine from glasses of friend and foe alike.

In 1907, the Nachtlicht moved and changed its name to the Fledermaus (bat). The locale was a Secessionist masterpiece, designed by the Wiener Werkstätte. One room had walls of hand-painted tiles depicting famous Viennese personalities. Elegance was the keynote. Programmes contained colour woodcuts by Kokoschka, and work by Gustav Klimt and Emil Orlik. For the opening night Kokoschka also created a shadow play in the French tradition, entitled 'The Spotted Egg'. The talent which the Fledermaus drew together was as great on the artistic as on the literary side.

Here Peter Altenberg produced sketches, monologues and poems and Egon Friedell recounted those humorous anecdotes which have become famous as they typify the Viennese spirit. A large number of these are reports of conversations between himself and Peter Altenberg.

Peter Altenberg said, 'You know, I am the only modern man who is truly hardy. On the coldest night, I sleep with my windows absolutely open.' To this I replied: 'That doesn't seem to be quite accurate. Last night I passed your house and all the windows were closed.' 'Well,' said Peter Altenberg, 'was yesterday's then the coldest night!?!'

Feuilletoniste, theatre critic, actor and author of among other things a massive cultural history of ancient and modern times, Egon Friedell was above all a satirist who mocked patriots, politicians, journalists, Zionists, Jewish assimilationists, left-wing and right-wing radicals, and all other conceivable ideas and organizations, as the actor Fritz Kortner notes in his memoirs. In the *Fledermaus* he collaborated to good effect with Alfred Polgar, another Viennese essayist and critic. Together they wrote a number of sketches and short dramas for the cabaret. One of the most celebrated of these was entitled 'Goethe' and was a repeated success for many years.

Goethe, played in impeccable Frankfurt accent by Freidell, appears in ghostly form to a student, highly nervous because he is about to sit an examination on this cultural totem. The great poet decides to take over the student's body and take the examination for him. What emerges is a marvellous parody of the pedantically academic Goethe cult. Goethe, of course, cannot answer the questions concerning dates put to him, since frankly whether one of his many

51

Opposite
Programme of the Budapester Orpheum.
Klaus Budzinski Archiv.

Cover of the Hölle Cabaret programme.
Klaus Budzinski Archiv.

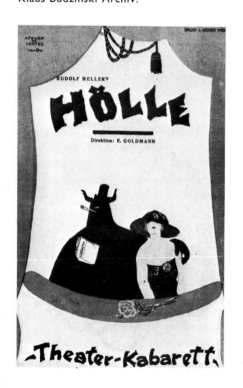

volumes of poetry appeared in 1776 or 1777 hardly seems significant to him. He tells the examiner off for meddling into his personal life. His interpretation of *Tasso* is deemed insulting and when he claims that his last words, 'More light' were actually a demand for more milk in his last cup of coffee, he is failed. The poor student, whose place he has taken, and who wanted to pass because he needed his doctorate in order to become a cabaretist, is left with only an autograph.

All of Egon Friedell's work contains that mixture of what Polgar characterized as the buffoon and the philosopher. He himself claimed that the philosopher begins to exist just at that juncture where the man ceases to take himself and life seriously. In 1938, when he saw SS troops coming through the door of his home, Friedell jumped to his death from a window. His personal history, linked with the particular philosophical humour of his writings, tells the story of an epoch.

Sandor Friedrich Rosenfeld, better known as Roda Roda, was another of Vienna's performing feuilletoniste. Although his attacks on militarism resulted in the banning of his plays on the Austro-Hungarian stage, much of his work is less polemical in character. Of his many anecdotes, one short one well encapsulates the turn of his humour, evident throughout his plays, novels, travelogues and Viennese stories. It is called 'The Post'.

One floor beneath me lives a Herr Robert Roder.

I, however, am called Roda Roda.

It sometimes happened that the postman read addresses too quickly and left my post at the downstairs flat. This Robert Roder would then regularly open my letters and send them up to me with an apology: In his haste, he had torn open the envelope, but he noticed from the very first few sentences that the letter belonged not to him but to me, and he begs . . . etc.

Yesterday, I had had enough of it. I asked my best friend to write me a letter with the opening words: 'You vulgar and noxious crocodile, you king of saps of both worlds and president of the Reich Association of Idiots . . .'

I sent this letter, opened, to Herr Roder with a card: 'Inadvertently, I accepted the enclosed letter – but from the very first line it was evident that it was meant for you, honoured Sir . . .' etc.

Robert Roder called me from across the stairs: he wished us to pay careful attention to addresses from now on.

The mark of the Vienna cabaret was its elegant humour and whimsy. Neither the Nachtlicht nor the Fledermaus were often partner to that acid wit of the German cabaret which confronted a sociopolitical reality. While the initial cabarets managed to walk the tightrope between artistry and kitsch, Vienna's later pre-war cabarets opted unconstrainedly for the latter. There were two notable exceptions, however: Die Hölle (Hell) which produced a real salonmephisto in Fritz Grünbaum, a conférencier who was admirably to

BUDAPESTER ORPHEUM-
GESELLSCHAFT
TÄGLICH
HÔTEL STEFANIE
II. BEZ.   TABORSTR. 12.
PROGRAMM

Director:
M. B. Lautzky.

Regisseur:
Heinrich Eisenbach.

Kapellmeister:
Art. Duchoslaw.

ENGAGIRTE MITGLIEDER:

Damen:

Risa Bastée   Lina Liebisch
Anna Eisenbach   Anna Violetta
Josefine Fischer   Paula Walden
Kathi Hornau   Leopoldine Werner

Herren:

Josef Bauer   Josef Koller
Heinr. Eisenbach   Albin Lukasch
Arthur Franzetti   Max Rott

Orchester und Chorpersonal.

The journalist Egon Erwin Kisch who participated in Prague's *Montmartre*, caricature by B. F. Dolbin in *Jugend*.

entertain post-war Germany; and the Budapester Orpheum. This latter cabaret was lauded by Kraus for the genius of its participants and their tragi-comic craft. It was composed mainly of Jewish comedians, some from Vienna, some from Budapest. In the tradition of the Viennese popular theatre, the Budapester's actors recreated, in a mixture of song, dance and sketches, the everyday life of the Jewish little man, constricted by his equals, yet quite lost without them.

Apart from being itself a multi-national state, Vienna was a gateway to the East. From here the cabaret moved to Hungary and Prague, where Jaroslav Hasek, creator of *The Good Soldier Schweik*, Franz Kafka, Max Brod and the political journalist Egon Erwin Kisch, regularly attended and sometimes contributed to the Montmartre cabaret, situated on the banks of the River Moldau. Hasek acted as satirical conférencier, Brod wrote sketches, and songs in Yiddish, Czech and German were sung, representing the various languages of the city.

It was Moscow, however, which had the most innovative eastern pre-war cabaret, named *Fledermaus* after its Vienna original. Many of the cabaretists were members of Stanislavsky's Moscow Art Theatre and they began by meeting in the basement of the theatre and improvising. Writers, actors, singers and composers, including Chaliapin and Rachmaninov, were members of the circle. Under the direction of Nikita Baliev, – who became a wittily cynical conférencier – the group called itself the Fledermaus, and moved into its own premises where it performed experimental theatre which Stanislavsky himself applauded. Bakst who was later to work for Diaghelev's Ballet Russe, was the Fledermaus designer.

54

Cabaret as a Meeting Place for Artists

Simplicissimus

The Ten Commandments of Cabaret Life

1. Come, if possible, late, so that the guests already there know that you *do* have something else to do.
2. Give your coat to the woman in the Cloakroom. You're a friendly man and your coat is new.
3. Sit down haphazardly and noisily. Then change your seat often until you find one with the right shape.
4. Read the menu and wine list loudly and noisily to your companion. Learn it if possible off by heart, and then order a portion of 'later'.
5. When everything concerning your material welfare has been looked after, take part — even if at first only unwillingly — in the artistic presentation. Look upon the conférencier with contempt right from the start. He's an ass and because of that, let him feel your spiritual superiority.
6. Place your loud interruptions exactly where they don't fit. This actually belongs to the enlivening of the programme.
7. If you're a woman, then criticize the dress of the performing artiste loudly and skilfully. (Don't forget your lorgnette for this.)
8. During song presentations, blow your smoke unbotheredly toward the podium. The singer will inhale it willingly. It makes his voice soft and supple.
9. During acts, use your cutlery and glasses in an unbothered fashion. Their sound does one good and replaces the band.
10. When you have been bored long enough by the programme and have gotten angry over the bill, leave as noisily as you came in with the consciousness of having spent a most enjoyable evening.

(from *Simplicissimus-Künstlerkneipe* ed. Réné Prévot)

The Simplicissimus dog, designed by Th. Th. Heine. Klaus Budzinski Archiv.

These rules of cabaret behaviour characterize the spirit of Munich's Schwabing or Schwabylon as it came to be known in the pre-war years. An anarchistic jollity prevailed, a desire to shock the establishment out of its conventional conformity. Its home was the Simplicisumus Künstlerkneipe.

The Simplicissimus cabaret (known as the Simpl') was a gathering place for poets, artists, political radicals and students — all those who were opposed to the official norms of cultural life in Wilhelmine Germany. It had originated in the Dichtelei, a drinking and talking

55

place which the Executioners' group had frequented. A stately, prepossessing waitress of peasant stock, presided here, Kathi Kobus by name. Beloved by her bohemians, Kathi was encouraged to open her own bistro. When she had found a locale and the necessary finances, her followers paraded along Türkenstrasse, centre of Schwabing, carrying her possessions and lighted candles. Wedekind led the group, strumming his guitar.

Kathi had wanted to call her new bistro the Neue Dichtelei, but her former boss objected to this and commenced proceedings against her. So Th. Th. Heine and Rudolf Wilke, caricaturists and members of the *Simplicissimus* magazine editorial board, suggested that the new locale be called after the magazine. And Simplicissimus it was to be, once Kathi, on her knees, had won over disapproving editor Albert Langen. Th. Th. Heine gave the new cabaret its emblem, a relative of the Simplicissimus bulldog in chains, a red bulldog joyfully opening a bottle of *sekt*.

The cabaret consisted of two rooms connected by a narrow hall, made even narrower by its profusion of tables and chairs. The walls were filled with paintings and drawings made by Kathi's artistic guests, who offered them either as payment for drinks or simply as gifts, in remembrance of delightful Simplicissimus nights. A small podium and piano made up the 'stage' in the back room, and here every night there was an informal programme of songs, poetry, music and occasionally dance. The performers were generally the creators of their own work, and all of them – apart, of course, from visiting notables – were Kathi's regular guests. Of the many anecdotes surrounding the Simpl', one tells of Isadora Duncan dancing in varying degrees of nudity on table-tops until the early hours of the morning.

Kathi had no formal ideas of what constituted talent, but her intuitions were excellent and the Simpl's guests always outnumbered the places available for them. Performers rarely earned themselves more than free drink and food, and the none-too-generous Kathi kept strict accounts. But this was enough for their near-empty bohemian pockets. And their fame spread beyond the doors of the Simpl' throughout Germany.

Here Mary Irber, one of the originals of Wedekind's Lulu, dressed in flimsy dresses to which the police often objected, sang Wedekind's song of the obedient girl:

> *Die Mutter sprach im ernsten Ton*
> *'Du zählst nun sechzehn Jahre schon,*
> *Drum, Herzblatt, nimm dich stets in acht,*
> *Besonders bei der Nacht!'*

> The mother spoke in earnest tone,
> 'You are sixteen, almost full grown,
> Therefore, loved one, do beware,
> Especially by night, tread with care!'

The poet Ludwig Scharf, for a time engaged to Kathi, was a regular too.

56

In those days, Scharf was known as the King of Bohemia. He had a wooden leg, and would stride to the middle of the room declaiming in a loud falsetto his 'Proleta Sum'.

> *Ich bin ein Prolet, vom Menschengetier*
> *Bin ich von der untersten Klasse.*
> *Ich bin ein Prolet, was kann ich dafür*
> *Wenn ich keine Zier eurer Rasse!*
>
> I am a prole, in the human heirarchy
> I am of the class most base.
> I am a prole, what can I do
> If I provide no honour to your race!

Kathi too, would perform. In her folksy Bavarian dress, she would call her guests to order and recite some of her own dialect poems. Totally unselfconscious, she kept her eyes on what was going on around her, and might stop in the middle of a line to call a waitress's attention to an unattended guest. She remained unflustered no matter what the nature of the brawls which took place, and there were many nights on which glasses were not the only things to be broken. A story about her recounts that one evening the crown prince and a young friend visited the Simpl' incognito. Kathi recognized the prince, but did not let on. When this noble guest and his friend deigned to be a little too rowdy and made a general nuisance of themselves during performance time, Kathi, quite unflustered, called the brawlers to order with one of her many dialect expletives: 'Saupreiss'n stad san!' – 'Shut up you Prussian sows!'

One of Kathi's admirers was the poet Joachim Ringelnatz, who said:

> *Es gibt in ganzen Globus,*
> *Nur ein Kathi Kobus!*
>
> There is in the entire globus,
> Only one Kathi Kobus!

Ringelnatz's name remains one of the central ones in the Simpl's history. He was born Hans Bötticher in Saxony, the son of a writer and artist. At eighteen he left his parental home to go to sea. Until his appearance some seven years later in Munich, he had wandered round the world, worked at odd jobs and spent some time – for lack of another shelter – in an Amsterdam jail. With a craggy profile, sailor's rolling gait, great capacity for drink and his adventurous past, Ringelnatz was a prize candidate for the Munich bohemia. Indeed, this 'Sinbad the Sailor of the soul' encapsulated the bohemian myth.

Ringelnatz recounts how he stumbled on the Simpl' one night and found the atmosphere so entrancing that he was drawn there constantly. A little shy of the artists and poets who sat at the favoured regulars' table, he always placed himself discreetly in a corner. One night, however, he built up enough courage to ask Kathi if he might

Above
Joachim Ringelnatz performing at the Simplicissimus. Klaus Budzinski Archiv.

Right
A Sailor's Tavern with Ringelnatz alias Kuttel-Daddeldu in left-hand corner. Drawing by Karl Arnold.

recite some lyrics. He did, but it proved a total failure. Then Ringelnatz went home and wrote his 'Simplicissimustraum', a poem which describes the cabaret, its guests and atmosphere. Success. From then on Ringelnatz performed nightly an ever-growing list of Simpl' or situational poems. And later he gave birth to, Kuttel-daddeldu, a wandering maritime balladeer who was his creator's persona. The Kuttel-daddeldu poems are some of Germany's best-loved, and when Ringelnatz recited or sang them in his swaying fashion friends testify that the walls of the room they were in drew back and the world poured in from all sides.

As 'house-poet' Ringelnatz did not really earn enough to live. Kathi's generosity did not extend much further than one mark for an evening and Ringelnatz, like his fellows, tended to drink his earnings. So he opened a tobacco shop near the Simpl' which he decorated outlandishly with his own drawings and travel mementoes. The Simpl' crowd often made their way here with song and music, but the neighbours complained and soon Ringelnatz, never an astute business-man, was forced to close down. Odd jobs again, and then during the

58

war, to sea. But even after the war, when his fame had spread by report and publication, Ringelnatz never earned enough from cabaret work to survive comfortably. He was constantly on the brink of disaster, like many of his bohemian fellows.

Ringelnatz's poems, beneath their lyrically playful surface, convey a deeply humanist position, a concern with those universals of life which are opposed to any forms of strutting nationalism or hypocritical morality. After the war he became a prolific contributor to the important left-wing intellectual magazine, *Die Weltbühne*. By the early twenties, he was already being attacked by the right-wing press and when the Nazis came to power in 1933, his works were banned and were not to be republished until 1951. This bohemian jack-of-all-trades, whose poems convey the language and feeling of the places he knew best – ships, the bars of international ports, fun fairs, working-class streets – was the prevailing spirit of the Simplicissimus.

However, of the members of the Simplicissimus bohemia, only one can unambiguously be termed a revolutionary: Erich Mühsam. He was one of the most acclaimed of the Simpl' poets and a cabaretist who performed in many locales across Europe. His aphoristic verse as well as his satirical songs and ballads set to music became staples of cabaret after the war. In all of his writings, which include political tracts, a history of the 1918 Munich uprising, drama, prose and verse, the socially committed purpose of his life is evident: 'Struggle, Revolution, Equality, Freedom,' as he himself put it.

He was the son of a Jewish Berlin pharmacist. When he was expelled from his Lübeck school for socialist agitation, he apprenticed himself to a pharmacist and travelled around Germany. By 1901 he was already launched as a freelance writer. Mühsam's politics were essentially anarchistic, or, as he called them, anarcho-communist. He fiercely believed in individual freedom and defended it whether it was being encroached upon from right or left. His socialism was of a kind which could never realize itself in a state, only in the on-going work of eradicating social injustice. Among his many causes were sexual emancipation and penal reform.

Mühsam's sharply turned aphorisms made him one of the Simpl's and indeed of Germany's most acute social critics outside of Wedekind. His comment upon his return from France to Germany has deservedly become famous: 'Paris lives. Berlin functions.' Bearded, with masses of red hair, and sporting raggedy clothes, Mühsam typifies our contemporary image of the revolutionary bohemian. In biting tones he would deliver one of his masterful 'Schwabing six-liners', a form he brought to satirical perfection and which loses a great deal in translation.

> *Es stand ein Mann am Siegestor,*
> *Der an ein Weib sein Herz verlor.*
> *Schaut sich nach ihr die Augen aus,*
> *In Händen einen Blumenstrauss.*
> *Zwar ist dies nichts Besunderes.*
> *Ich aber – ich bewundere' es.*

There stands a man at Victory gate[1]
Who lost his heart to a common Kate.
Stared his eyes out at her night and day,
In his hands a large bouquet.
Nothing extraordinary about it.
I, but I, do wonder at it.

Mühsam's political satires set the tone for the post-war politically committed writers. Indeed his 'Der Revoluzzer', suprisingly written as early as 1907, became one of the most performed chansons of the Weimar Republic, where the gap between political action and paper social democracy had grown to the size of a chasm into which Germany would plunge towards Nazism. The translation here, by John Burgess, is a recreation of the acidly satirical original.

War einmal ein Revoluzzer,
im Zivilstand Lampenputzer;
ging im Revoluzzerschritt
mit den Revoluzzern mit.

Und er schrie: 'Ich revolüzze!'
Und die Revoluzzermütze
schob er auf das linke Ohr,
kam, sich höchst gefärlich vor.

Doch die Revoluzzer schritten
mitten in der Strassen Mitten,
wo er sonsten unverdrutzt
alle Gaslaternen putzt.

Sie vom Boden zu entfernen,
rupfte man die Gaslaternen
aus dem Strassenpflaster aus,
zwecks des Barrikadenbaus.

Aber unser Revoluzzer
schrie: 'Ich bin der Lampenputzer
dieses guten Leuchtelichts.
Bitte, bitte, tut ihm nichts!

Wenn wir ihn' das Licht ausdrehen,
kann kein Bürger nichts mehr sehen.
Lasst die Lampen stehn, ich bitt! –
Denn sonst spiel ich nicht mehr mit!'

Doch die Revoluzzer lachten,
und die Gaslaternen krachten,
und der Lampenputzer schlich
fort und weinte bitterlich.

Dann ist er zu Haus geblieben
und hat dort ein Buch geschrieben:
nämlich, wie man revoluzzt
und dabei doch Lampen putzt.

[1] A Munich gate.

He cleaned the gas lamps on the street,
That's what he did to make ends meet,
The rest of the time it was a different story,
This lad, you see, was a Revolutionary.

He talked revolution day and night,
Shouted, 'Power to the People' with all his might.
He pushed his beret over one ear
And swore he'd sell his life so dear.

The revolutionaries marched down the middle of the street,
The houses shook to their marching feet,
While all along the pavements gleamed
The brave gas lamps our hero cleaned.

But the marchers had designs
On those polished lamps so fine.
'Quick, pull them down,' the leader said,
'We'll use them for a barricade.'

'Oh please don't touch, oh can't you see,
Those lamp-posts mean so much to me.'
He begged, he pleaded, he cajoled,
When all else failed, he then grew bold . . .

'Leave them alone. If they don't work
you'll leave the bourgeois in the dark!
If you will behave in this reckless way,
Then I'm no longer going to play.'

The others simply roared with laughter
And took the lamp posts they were after,
While our hero slunk away,
Sat in a corner and began to cry.

After this he stayed at home,
Working on a learned tome
On 'How to overthrow society
While treating lamp-posts with due propriety.'

Mühsam's satire grew out of a deep belief in the possibility of change
and to this he actively dedicated his life. By the time World War I
broke out, he was a revolutionary pacifist who refused even to carry
out alternate labour service. When it is considered how the World
War brought even a great many reputed 'socialists' to nationalistic
fervour, Mühsam's presence of mind seems remarkable. He paid the
price of his pacifism by being sentenced to gaol in the Traunstein
fortress in Bavaria.

In that chaotic year of 1918–19 – filled with strikes, mass action and
succession of governments – when Germany's political future was
being decided, Mühsam played a significant role in Bavaria's revolutionary uprisings. Along with the poet Ernst Toller and the philosopher Gustav Landauer, he was responsible for the establishment of
the short-lived Bavarian Soviet Republic. This was a government by
poets which succeeded Kurt Eisner's tragic assassination, and was

Th. Th. Heine's version of Munich's 'Red' Ideologists. The caption reads: Communism is only possible when everyone is an ideal person. I believe that you will all fulfil this precondition.' *Simplicissimus*, 1919.

itself replaced by Eugen Leviné's Communist Party executive.

By June 1919 the various revolutionary regimes with their idealistic aspirations were at an end. The independent Soviet Republic had had a brief existence, but the retributions which followed from it were to extend through the next decade. Landauer was brutally murdered; Leviné, the KPD leader, executed. The policy of the central Social Democratic government was to rely heavily on the army which in turn mobilized the brutal, right-wing Free Corps to help put down the 'Red rising'. The result was 6000 dead in Bavaria. 4000 people were imprisoned, and Mühsam, being one of the most hated of the revolutionaries, was sentenced by a Bavarian tribunal to fifteen years. Ironically, after the Munich putsch Hitler was incarcerated in the same fortress.

While Hitler produced *Mein Kampf* within its walls, Mühsam wrote a proletarian drama, *Judas*, accounts of his revolutionary experience, and many songs and poems, one of which became extremely popular. Called 'The Death of the Red Guard Soldier', this song is based on Mühsam's witnessing the death of a young fellow combattant during the uprising. Its theme is the idealistic ardour which bravely serves the revolutionary cause and it ends with these words, spoken by the dying revolutionary.

> *Ihr könnt, ob ich selbst auch verloren bin,*
> *Den Glauben mir nicht entreissen:*
> *Ich sterbe, doch am Leben bliebt*
> *Die Revolution!*

> Even if you kill me,
> My belief continues to thrive.
> I myself may die, but
> the revolution remains alive.

Social Democrat election poster of 1932. Directed against the Nazis, it shows a worker crucified on a swastika.

When there was a general amnesty in 1924, Mühsam was one of the last prisoners to be released. He returned to radical activity, now highly politicized, but still maintained his essentially anarchist position and criticized infringements of liberty by both left and right. He was well-known by the Nazis because of his many public and cabaret appearances, his new translation of 'The International', and his writings, and became one of the first victims of Hitler's take-over. On the night of the burning of the Reichstag, Mühsam was arrested by the SS, just four hours before a planned flight to Prague, a flight which had been postponed for lack of money. He was dragged from concentration camp to concentration camp, and was beaten and tortured. When she was allowed to visit him his wife could not recognize him.

Finally he was murdered, perhaps not even so much for his writings as for his last act of courage in standing up to the Nazis. When foreign journalists came to Camp Sonnenburg, the camp commander wanted to demonstrate how prisoners were kept here unharmed. Grouped together in a room, the prisoners were asked to tell the journalists whether anything not in order had been done to them. No one moved. Then Mühsam pulled his shirt and jacket off and pointed to a deep scissor wound on his chest which had been inflicted by a sadistic guard. His last days were spent in Camp Oranienburg. On 9 July 1933 he was taken to the camp commander. When he returned he told his fellow prisoners, 'They want me to hang myself, but I won't give them that pleasure.' On 10 July he was told by the commander that if he did not hang himself, it would be done for him. It was. The next morning he was found hanging. Witnesses say that the knot around his neck had been so well tied that the half-blind Mühsam could never have done it himself.

Mühsam's history takes us into the problem-fraught post-war epoch in which the best of German cabaret was radically politicized and vented bitter satire in protest against social and political evils. However, before it was transformed into a weapon for dissent, the cabaret established its position as a medium of the cultural avant-garde.

63

External sign board of the Lapin Agile, painted by André Gill. Musée du vieux Montmartre.

Le Lapin Agile: Salon of the avant-garde

By the time the century had turned, the cabaret had been in existence in Paris for some twenty years. Throughout its history it had served both as a centre for spectacle and as a meeting place for artists. Now, in these years whose imaginative exuberance was to give direction to art for the next half-century, the cabaret became increasingly a salon for the avant-garde, a place where ideas were hatched, and hoaxes concocted.

The cabaret was a natural environment for the avant-garde. Spectacle was of its essence, and the avant-garde needed to make a spectacle of itself in order to be heard. Its artistic dissent paralleled the cabaret's parody of entrenched values, both social and artistic. Humour – ranging in kind from a comic childlikeness to biting satire – marked both; and both seriously exploited the popular elements in art. Finally, the nature of the cabaret programme, its discontinuity supplemented by ironical commentary, reflected the basic composition of the experimental work. This kinship of cabaret and the early twentieth-century avant-garde was a two-way dynamic: one created the other and was in turn influenced by it.

The painters and writers who flocked to the cheap living quarters of Montmartre at the turn of the century extended the definition of artist so that it incorporated the entirety of the individual's life-habits. Following in the notorious footsteps of Rimbaud and Ubu-Jarry, their lives became as much an example of their art as the works they produced. Their pranks, their banquets and festivities, had the same imaginative source as their poems and paintings. With a humorous élan, they interiorized the cabaret spectacle and lived it out on life's stage. And the main headquarters for the planning of far-ranging artistic schemes was Le Lapin Agile.

Situated at the junction of the steeply-sloping rue St Vincent and the rue des Saules, just across from the cemetery where some three hundred Communards lay buried, the Lapin Agile is still much unchanged today, though its clientele has become one of museum hunters rather than artists. In the Symbolist period, the locale was called Le Cabaret des Assassins, suggesting the nature of many of its frequenters. Purchased by Aristide Bruant, who wished to preserve this landmark from the rapidly encroaching city, its speculators and inflationary prices, the cabaret became the Lapin Agile when a punning painter, A. Gill, created a signboard for it consisting of a large rabbit popping out of a frying pan: Là peint A. Gill or the Lapin Agile.

The cabaret was leased from Bruant by Frédéric Gerard, known as Frédé, a kindly, hirsute, guitar-touting inhabitant of the Butte, who freely extended credit to his impoverished artistic customers. For some ten years the cabaret served as a central meeting ground for artists, some of whom tower in the annals of European art, others who have been forgotten except in the obscure pages of memoirs: Picasso, Apollinaire, Max Jacob, Francic Carco, André Warnod, Utrillo, Pierre Mac Orlan, Roland Dorgelès Marie Laurencin, André Salmon, Jules Dépaquit, and Joachim Raphael Boronalis. The path to fame of

this last artist testifies to the imaginative ingenuity of the Lapin Agile group.

The writer, Roland Dorgelès, later to become an established literary figure, was then a struggling artist well-known on the Butte for his red sweater and tight-fitting black jacket which gave him the air of a 'grasshopper in mourning' – and for his pranks. Dorgelès had decided to settle a score with the Cubists, who were 'on and off' members of the Lapin Agile circle. He considered that the Cubists had become a pretentious bunch, and furthermore, their chief spokesman, Apollinaire, refused to answer any queries or criticisms of the movement. In order to mock the Cubists and to prove how easy it was to achieve fame in fashion-conscious Paris, Dorgelès invented an artist called Boronali, who declared himself head of a new artistic school: Excessivism. Boronali published a manifesto proclaiming the aims of the school. The manifesto was a perfect parody of Futurist prose and, given the Italian name of its inventor, seemed quite believable to the Paris public. Having launched a controversy about the merits of all the painterly 'isms', Dorgelès went in search of his artist.

The Lapin Agile's Frédé, who looked like a cross between a Canadian trapper and a Corsican bandit, kept a donkey called Lolo, an essential addition to the cabaret's rustic ambience. It was in this donkey that Dorgelès found his fashionable artist. Having discovered his 'artist', Dorgelès made a bet with all his 'snob' friends and those present at the Lapin that at the next Salon des Indépendants he would exhibit a painting more original and provocatively revolutionary than any other.

View of the Lapin Agile. Bibliothèque historique de la ville de Paris.

65

Frédé and the donkey, Lolo. Musée du vieux Montmartre.

In the presence of a bailiff brought to witness the proceedings, a paint brush was tied to Lolo's tail, and tubes of paint of different colours provided. Frédé looked on warning that his good donkey was not to be harmed. Lolo was fed capaciously and his natural response to a hearty dinner was to wag his tail. As Lolo wagged, the paint brush dipped into a variety of colours did its work on a large canvas held by André Warnod. Gradually the canvas assumed some rather curious and not uninteresting effects. The next step was to find a name for the painting, and after some discussion Dorgelès came up with the title which was to set the Paris critics talking: *Et le soleil se couche sur l'Adriatique* (And the sun sets on the Adriatic), by Joachim Raphael Boronali.

Lolo's masterwork was finished just in time for the Salon des Indépendants, and Dorgelès placed himself discreetly near the painting in order to hear the reactions of the spectators. They were exactly what he had breathlessly hoped for. The public and the critics, most of whom mentioned the work in their reviews, were divided as to the

66

value of the painting, but their comments on it did not differ appreciably in kind from those directed at the work of Van Dongen, Matisse and Roualt, all of whom exhibited at the same Salon. Dorgelès was ready to launch his bombshell. He told the papers of his hoax and the headlines read: 'Un Âne, Chef d'École' 'Donkey Heads Artistic School'. Lolo was a sensation! The Salon had never had so many visitors . . .

As Dorgelès reminisces, the Salon's new viewers could still not distinguish which painting belonged to the donkey Boronali, and which had been executed by the future greats of the century. A score of potential buyers appeared and Lolo, with a few swishes of his tail, became a very rich artist, not to mention an immortal one. Benezit unknowingly notes him in his reference work on painting as an Italian painter. Legend has it that during the World War, several years after he had been celebrated by the Paris *beau monde*, Lolo – bored by his country retirement home – committed suicide in the river of Saint-Cyr-sur-Morin. Like a true artist 'in a fit of neuresthenia'.

Dorgelès's pranks tested the supposed connoisseurship of the artistic world, sending up the hypocrisies of fashionable taste. They signalled that emphasis on vivid originality which was both the genius and occasionally the fraudulence of the avant-garde. Pranks – artistic gestures or artistic products – none, the avant-garde proved, could be met with the usual set of evaluative criteria and thus stand accounted for. Another of Dorgelès artistic activities gives an example of the inventive disruptiveness of the Montmartre group, In order to unveil the idiocy of apparent art-lovers, Dorgelès smuggled a bust, sculpted by a friend, into the Louvre's antique gallery. No one noticed the unusualness of this presence amongst the world's acclaimed 'classics' until Dorgelès and his friend arrived one day to claim it. Paris was scandalized both by Dorgelès and its own lack of perception.

It is no wonder then that in a climate rife with such hoaxes, the emergence of Cubism might be suspected as another ingenious fraud perpetrated by the half-starved dreamers of the Butte. Indeed Cubism could be seen as one of the spectacles invented within the precincts of the *Lapin Agile*, a humorous antic which, like so many in the tradition of modernism, grew into a serious imaginative project. At the turn of the century the distance between the Lapin and the famed Bateau Lavoir – a sprawling ramshackle residence, named for its resemblance to washerwomen's barges, which housed Picasso and Max Jacob and entertained some of the greatest talents of the century – was as short as the difference between ingenious hoaxes and significant artistic discoveries.

In his *De Montmartre au Quartier Latin*, Francis Carco recounts how the Lapin Agile served as the imaginative laboratory of modernism. Here the poet and impressario of the avant-garde, Guillaume Apollinaire, held forth on a variety of subjects: pure poetry, Negro art, Cubism and Orphism. Here the mathematician Princet introduced his artist friends to the 'mathematics of the fourth dimension'. Here Picasso is said to have uttered, '*Lorsque tu fais un paysage, il faut d'abord que ça ressemble à une assiete.*' (When you create a landscape, it must first of all resemble a plate.) And here too an important encounter with primitive African art took place. Max Jacob's brother, known as the 'explorer', came back from Africa with a portrait of himself. The group immediately noticed that Max's brother's golden jacket buttons were not where they should realistically have been, but situated in halo formation around his head. This discovery of the dissociation of objects may have inspired Picasso's statement soon afterwards, '*Si tu peins un portrait, tu mets les jambes à côté sur la toile.*' (If you paint a portrait, you place the legs next to it on the canvas.)

The Lapin Agile served as a salon not only for the new art, but also of literature. Pierre Mac Orlan, later to write *Quai des Brumes*, frequented the cabaret when he was not away on fortune-seeking ventures to the four corners of the globe. Dressed either as a cowboy or an English sportsman, he would recount those humorous anecdotes of adventure which shape his narrative style. These monologues were part of the Lapin's spectacle.

Max Jacob, mystic and humorist, who earned his living telling fortunes in fashionable salons, was a constant participant in the Lapin's evenings. The two rhymes he inscribed in Frédé's guestbook reveal that whimsical play-on-words which foreshadows surrealism.

> *9 heures du soir*
>
> *Trouver la rime à Frédéric,*
> * Voilà le hic!*
> *J'aime mieux attendre d'être ivre*
> *Pour m'inscrire à bord de ton livre.*
>
> *2 heures du matin*
>
> *A bord? Piano A. Bord.*
> * Livre de bord!*
> *Paris, la mer qui pense, apporte*
> *Ce soir au coin de ta porte*
> *O tavernier du quai des Brumes,*
> *Sa gerbe d'écume.*

A translation cannot hope to capture Jacob's clever puns, verbal and imagistic associations: 'à bord' means on board as well as at the edge, here of a book. A.Bord is also the name of a French piano firm. By playing on these associations, and stressing drunkenness, Jacob arrives at the image of the sea and its drunken motion.

> 9 in the evening
> To find a rhyme for Frédéric,
> That's the hic!
> I'd rather wait to be in a drunken state
> To register aboard your book.
>
> 2 in the morning
> On board! Piano A. Bord.
> Logbook!

> The sea, which thinks, brings
> This evening to the edge of your door
> O publican of the Quai des Brumes,
> Its bundle of sea-scum.

Less well-known now, the poet Jules Depaquit was also a regular at the *Lapin*. He would always hide himself away in sombre corners, unseen unless one moved numerous objects to get to him. Suddenly, out of this obscurity, he would begin reciting a song about a street organ in a rusty, groaning, yet comical voice.

> *C'est la musique incomprise,*
> *Qui fait vomir et qui grise et qui tue . . .*
> *A la fin on s'y habitue.*
>
> It's music which isn't understood,
> It makes one tipsy and grey and vomit away,
> And it kills . . .
> At the end one gets used to it.

Depaquit was the bard of mediocre dramas and the petty annoyances of existence. He sang of the obscure and ridiculous; and called his volume of poems, *Les moments perdus*, lost moments, since as he said, no editor has wanted to find them. Depaquit's lack of self-confidence, his timid little man's approach to life is evident in this anecdote which is told about his visit to Alphonse Allais. Apparently Allais, impressed by his work, had invited him to call for lunch. However, when the concierge of the building asked him his business and he replied he wished to see Allais, she sent him to the servants' entrance. The cook answered the door and after Depaquit had announced his name, she told him that it was a bad moment to call, since Allais had an important luncheon date. Depaquit was asked to wait in the kitchen. The servants were agitated because Allais's guest did not seem to be arriving and they proceeded to serve the meal. Finally Depaquit was invited to share the servants' food and when Madame Allais came into the kitchen and asked who he was, he whispered, 'I didn't want to disturb anyone . . .' Personally unprepossessing, Depaquit did however gradually win acclaim on the Butte for the persistent excellence of his verse and its bitter wit.

Francis Carco, whose numerous books provide an almost daily chronical of life on Montmartre, was perhaps the Lapin's most devoted frequenter. Having come to Paris like so many others, a poor provincial in search of a place in the artistic world, he found in the *Lapin* both a refuge and a stimulant to artistic activity. The business of earning one's living was never very easy for these young artists and often Frédé would generously provide them with their only sustenance for the day. The poverty of these bohemians was often as great as that of the other clients of the Lapin — vagrants, rogues, petty criminals, with the girls they had picked up at the Moulin de la Galette or at one of the numerous 'bals' of the Butte. Indeed, it was often mere chance which distinguished between those who would leave

Poster by Roedel advertising one of Montmartre's many dance halls, The Moulin de la Galette. Bibliothèque historique de la ville de Paris.

their names in the annals of art from those who would end up in police files.

Meanwhile, the Lapin provided antics, gaiety, poetry, song and discussion. Walls were filled with the works of the frequenters: Utrillo, who sketched for drink; a blue period Picasso harlequin; a large Christ sculpted by Wasley, which served as a coatrack. From time to time Bruant would drop in and sing, and on evenings of exhibition openings the whole group would gather and talk into the small hours of the morning.

But danger and an underlying despair were never far away. The poet, Gaston Couté, author of *Chansons d'un gars qu'a mal tourné*,

70

could often be seen lying dead drunk on a bench, and his occasional groans would remind the group of their own situation. Frédé's pistol was always at hand and his songs, with their mixture of dream and desolation, might be interrupted by shots ringing through the window. For the most part poets and vagrants got on well. Occasionally, however, those 'guests' whom Frédé had refused entry would unload their pistols on the Lapin. One such outburst of violence resulted in the death of Frédé's son, Victor.

Victor was idolized by all the girls who came to the Lapin and they would entangle themselves in a variety of escapades to win his love. Their men were jealous, and it was probably by one such jealous lover that Victor was murdered one night. Frédé never quite recovered from the shock. Indeed, in many ways Victor's death signalled the end of an era. Many of the Montmartre regulars led by Apollinaire, began leaving the Butte for the Quartier Latin. The time for youthful escapades was over and with them the playful cabaretistic spirit of the Lapin Agile passed away. War was on the horizon.

But the cabaret had served as headquarters of an epoch in which, as Apollinaire testified, 'We learned to laugh.'

The interior of the Lapin Agile. In the background, Picasso's *Harlequin*. Musée du vieux Montmartre.

Cabaret as a Vehicle of the Artistic Vanguard

Futurist Performance

If the Lapin Agile developed quite unintentionally into a planning centre for artistic hoaxes, in the rest of Europe avant-garde artistic movements self-consciously paralleled the *gestus* or style of cabaret. Although these groups did not always find their setting in an actual cabaret, they used its modes as an important element in their revolutionary intent.

In Italy the Futurist Filippo Tommaso Marinetti defined a new kind of performance medium based on the variety show. The Variety Theatre, according to his 1913 manifesto on the subject, provided a useful model because it was 'fed by swift actuality'; it wished 'to distract and amuse the public with comic effects, erotic stimulation, or imaginative astonishment'. By breaking down the boundaries between audience and performers; by incorporating the smoke and noise of the audience into the 'entertainment'; by encouraging laughter at the 'worn-out prototypes of the Beautiful, the Grand, the Solemn, the Religious, the Ferocious, the Seductive and the Terrifying, the Variety Theatre . . . destroys the Solemn, the Sacred, the Serious, and the Sublime in Art with a capital A.'

More radical in his anti-traditionalist stand, Marinetti yet duplicated the intent of the early German cabaretists. Popular culture, with its variety, its excitement, its humour, is to be appropriated by 'artists' for the purpose of serious artistic experiment and socio-political critique. The illusory, yet persistent, fourth wall of the conventional stage was to be broken down. Actors were not to play *to each other* and maintain the fiction of a reality existing on stage, but were to play to their audience and provoke it into participation. So too the cabaret, by making artists their own performers, by introducing an improvisational commentary on action and events, and by creating an intimacy between 'stage' and spectator, challenged the traditional division between performance and audience.

Given this structural kinship, Futurist performance went beyond the contemporary cabaret both in its sheer aggression and in its radical experimentation. Following Marinetti's suggestions for inducing surprise and participation from spectators – such as spreading powerful glue on the seats, or selling the same ticket to ten people – the Futurists provoked riots which were only to be equalled in violence by their heirs, the Dadaists. The *serate*, or evenings, they engineered in galleries or theatres provided a mixture of art – carried

72

or attached to walls – music, poetry, sketches, polemics, and quasi-political action. Manifestoes were generally declaimed by a number of members, outlandishly costumed, and moving as they spoke. They were accompanied by the sound of home-made musical instruments which produced what conventional composers would call 'noise' and what became known as 'bruitism', the art of noise. The sketches or plays – examples of synthetic theatre – were intensely brief distillations of traditional drama, always anti-naturalistic, sometimes humorous, sometimes merely startlingly evocative images. Examples are Francesco Cangiullo's *Detonation: Synthesis of all modern theatre*:

Character
A Bullet

Road at night, cold deserted.
A minute of silence. – A gunshot.
CURTAIN

or *Negative Act* by Bruno Corra and Emilio Settimelli:

A Man enters, busy, preoccupied. He takes off his overcoat, his hat, and walks furiously.
Man: What a fantastic thing! Incredible! (He turns toward the public, is irritated to see them, then coming to the apron, says categorically) I . . . I have absolutely nothing to tell you . . . Bring down the curtain!
CURTAIN

73

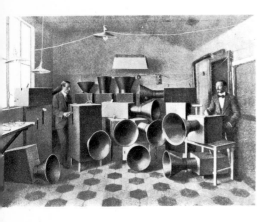

Luigi Russolo with his noise organ. From a photograph in *L'Arte de Rumori*, Milan 1916.

The variety of scenographic effects devised by the Futurists — especially their brilliant designer, Enrico Prampolini — their experimentation with actor-free performance composed only of light and sound effects, still retain their startling quality. But they bring us beyond the bounds of cabaret which — whatever the nature of its avant-garde theatrical innovations — always gives primary place to the live immediacy of the performer's presence.

The Early Expressionists

A different kind of artistic experimentation was taking place in Berlin between 1909 and 1910. A group of young poets, writers and publicists were meeting in the back rooms of cafés or bookshops, far from the jeering eyes of 'philistines', and performing, reading, discussing their work with one another. This group, later to take on the name 'Expressionists', initially included Kurt Hiller, Jakob van Hoddis, and Erich Unger amongst others, and was linked to the famous expressionist magazines *Der Sturm* and *Die Aktion*. By 1910 the group had decided to make its performances public, and calling itself the Neopathetische Cabaret it held demonstration evenings in various locales around Berlin. On its opening night Kurt Hiller explained the reasoning behind the cabaret's name:

> Pathos not as a grave gesture of suffering prophets' sons, but as universal celebration, a Pan-like laughter . . . We find it in no way unworthy or vulgar to scatter philosophy between songs and witticisms. On the contrary, it is especially because philosophy for us is not an academic discipline, but something with vital meaning . . . an experience, that it seems to us infinitely more suitable to cabaret than to a lecturing desk or quarterly journal. But these last words already sound like an attempt at justification . . . They don't dance self-assuredly like that merry play of intellect we seek. Therefore I close my address and open the Neopathetische Cabaret for adventurers of the spirit.

Despite this evocation of the cabaret's laughing spirit — which for the time was synonymous with being modern — the Neopathetische was strictly a high-brow artistic society. Self-consciously modernist, the cabaret served as a performance vehicle for the new literature of the time and became the stage of early Expressionism. It is difficult now to recapture the impact a poem like Jakob van Hoddis's 'End of the World' (Weltende) had on its contemporary audience:

> The bourgeois's hat flies off his pointed head,
> The air re-echoes with a cry.
> Roofers plunge and hit the ground,
> And at the coast — one reads — seas are rising.

74

The storm is here, the savage seas hop
On land and crash thick dams.
Most people have a cold.
Trains fall off bridges.

According to Johannes R. Becher, this poem which was repeated over and over, sung, chanted, hummed, had a metamorphic effect on its contemporary listeners. Its dissonant, fragmentary nature, its positing of a simultaneity of events, appeared as the very voice of the modern metropolis. And van Hoddis, himself, dwarf-like, unshaven, bedraggled, insane from 1914 to 1942, seemed the emanation of the city's spirit.

The Neopathetische evenings included poetry, by among others Else Lasker-Schüler, the great actress Tilla Durieux speaking Wedekind, shadow plays and music by Schönberg and Debussy. Van Hoddis and Hiller quarrelled, and the group split in two, with Hiller forming the Cabaret Gnu in 1911. The fact that the poet Georg Heym was discovered and almost forced into the limelight by these cabarets indicates their innovative importance. Heym was the poet who perhaps most vividly fulfilled the Expressionist insistence on vision, on the ability to capture what lay 'beyond' the brutalizing facts of the city with its factories, disease, prostitutes, poverty and general misery. Modelling himself on Van Gogh and on his favourite poet, Rimbaud, Heym exploded the ordinary into the surreal. Square and clumsy, a prole among aristocrats, as early as 1911 George Heym evoked the coming of war which he, like the Futurists and many of his own circle, welcomed. The terrors of war would, it was felt, shatter banality. But Heym, drowned in the Wannsee in 1912, was spared the practical outcome of his apolitical visionary politics.

Others were not. Yet initially the outbreak of war was met by nearly everyone with jubilation. The world seemed to be caught in a frenzy of self-destructive madness and only one small European nation provided a shelter of sanity for dissidents and pacifists.

The World as Dada cabaret

Zurich, the Noah's Ark of World War I. International centre for emigrés: those who objected to war outright, and those who had had some experience of the front and were fleeing its butchery. At various periods during those years, Zurich played host to James Joyce, Stephan Zweig, Romain Rolland, Lenin and Krupskaya, to name only the most illustrious. Along with the others came a young German poet, Hugo Ball, who had been acquainted with Berlin's early Expressionist circles, Munich's theatre groups and Kandinsky's Blaue Reiter school. In 1914 Ball had volunteered for war service, but quickly recognized the unheroic nature of battle, and was discharged after half a year for health reasons. He fled to Zurich with his mistress, the singer and poet, Emmy Hennings, and there, in 1916, he convinced Herr Ephraim, the owner of a somewhat seedy bar, the Meierei, to permit him to run a cabaret on his premises. Herr Ephraim's motivation was Ball's promise that the sales of beer, sausage and rolls would rise dramatically with the help of a literary cabaret.

This is how the Cabaret Voltaire was born. Voltaire, that great enlightener could smile his loftily ironical smile of reason on the madness of war; but since his 'reason' had degenerated into the common sense of the burgher and led to the irrationality of war, the goings-on in the Cabaret Voltaire would experiment with a new kind of unreason in order to develop a sanity more appropriate to the moment. The tactics — illuminism — were the same, the means radically different.

After a successful opening night for the Cabaret Voltaire, on which Emmy Hennings sang *chansons* by Bruant and others accompanied by Ball at the piano, Ball inserted the following announcement in a number of Zurich newspapers.

Cabaret Voltaire. Under this name a group of young artists and writers has formed with the object of becoming a centre for artistic entertainment. The Cabaret Voltaire will be run on the principle of daily meetings where visiting artists will perform their music and poetry. The young artists of Zurich are invited to bring along their ideas and contributions.

Almost overnight there gathered a group of young artists and poets, from everywhere in Europe, and the cabaret was filled to overflowing. Hans Arp, painter and poet, contributed his own graphic work, as well as some Picassos, to the cabaret's decor; Marcel Janco, a Romanian artist, donated huge archangels which stood out significantly amidst Futurist posters; Tristan Tzara was there, the poet whose untiring energy was to be one of the driving forces of the movement. The Ukranian, Marcel Slodki, designed the poster for the Cabaret Voltaire.

As if by magic, a movement was born: Dada. Who invented the name? What did it mean? The answers are as different as the members of the group. Dada, the Slavic affirmation, a grand 'yes' to life and to freedom? Dada, 'c'est mon dada', the French hobbyhorse, an individualized pursuit for individualistic enthusiasts? Dada, daddy? Dadadadada, a madcap, nonsense syllable, a child-like discarding of any attributable meaning? Dada was all these things, an incarnation of the unsystematizable spirit of creativity. If defied the conventional art of museums, rebelled against history and that art and language which, perhaps unintentionally, had played into the hands of warmakers, and it shocked the good Swiss burghers. If it propagated anything, it was liberation through laughter. It blossomed in the Cabaret Voltaire, and bore fruit throughout Europe and America.

Some thirty-two years after the event Hans Arp wrote in *Dadaland*:

Revolted by the butchery of the 1914 World War, we in Zurich devoted ourselves to the arts. While the guns rumbled in the distance, we sang, painted, made collages, and wrote poems with

Opposite
Cabaret Voltaire by Marcel Janco. Zurich 1916. Courtesy Marcel Janco.

76

Dada dancers. Courtesy Mrs Hans Arp.

Dada-merika by Grosz and Heartfield, 1919.

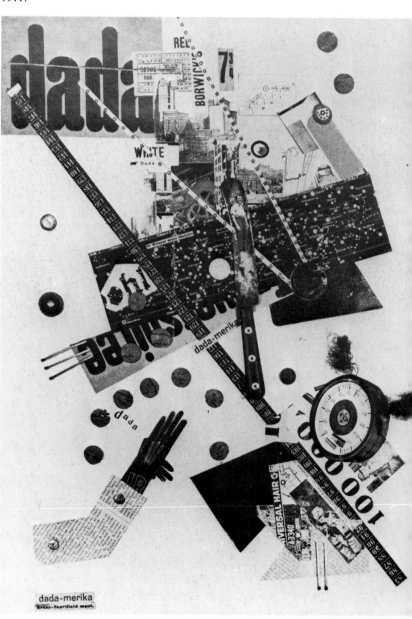

78

all our might. We were seeking an art based on fundamentals, to cure the madness of the age, and a new order of things that would restore the balance between heaven and hell. We had a dim premonition that power-mad gangsters would one day use art itself as a way of deadening men's minds.

The Dadaists wanted to create an art which was anti-war and negated the very spirit that had produced war. What they created at the most fundamental level was life: a boisterous, extravagant series of happenings. Like life at its highest pitch, their art represented a constant process of creation. In the cabaret the Dadaists found for a brief moment their natural environment and vehicle. Pictures were not meant to be gazed at with exalted awe in dusty museums, but to be part of an intimate space in which one lived, laughed and shouted. Books were objects from which their makers had departed, leaving only the dead letter of language. Theatre was a state institution in which one politely applauded distant creatures who mouthed the sentiments of others. But the cabaret was alive: creators were physically present as performers, close to spectators who could be provoked into becoming part of the spectacle at any moment. The programme itself was an unsystematic collage whose various pieces could be randomly rearranged and altered, in an ongoing process of creation.

Hugo Ball reciting 'gadji beri bimba'. Cabaret Voltaire 1916. Kunsthaus Zurich.

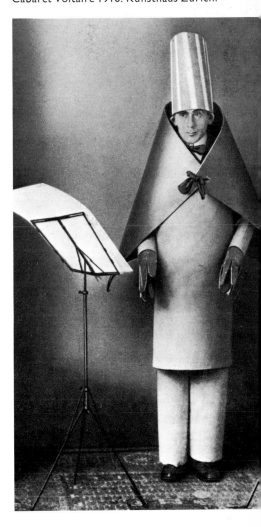

So the Cabaret Voltaire staged a disparate programme: performances by French, Russian, German and Swiss poets and writers; songs by Bruant; a balalaika orchestra; Rubenstein playing Saint-Saëns; poems by Max Jacob, Erich Mühsam, van Hoddis; the auctioning of a doll. Any variety of combinations was possible. And of course, as the days passed there were the personal creations of the Dadaists themselves. Hans Richter, who joined the Dadaists in August 1916, describes Tristan Tzara's performances in this way:

He declaimed, sang, and spoke in French, although he could do so just as well in German, and punctuated his performances with screams, sobs and whistles. Bells, drums, cow-bells, blows on the table or on empty boxes, all enlivened the already wild accents of the new poetic language, and excited, by purely physical means, an audience which had begun by sitting impassively behind its beer-mugs. From this state of immobility it was roused into frenzied involvement with what was going on. This was Art, this was Life, and this was what they wanted!

The Cabaret Voltaire performance was one marked by audience provocation and protest. Surprise or shock tactics, the use of bruitistic elements, poetry or prose which was aggressively anti-logical, experiments with masks, costuming and dance which were radically anti-conventional – all these played a part in the Dadaists' unprogrammed attempt to liberate the imagination from the shackles of tradition. Tristan Tzara wrote in one of his manifestoes: 'I smash drawers, those of the brain and those of social organizations; everywhere to demoralize, to hurl the hand from heaven to hell, the eyes from hell to heaven, to

79

set up once more, in the real powers and in the imagination of every individual, the fecund wheel of the world circus.'

If the Cabaret Voltaire was an imaginative circus, then the poet and psychiatrist, Richard Hülsenbeck, was its ringmaster. As Richter recounts, the arrogant Hülsenbeck would chant his '*Phantastische Gebete*' (Fantastic Prayers) accompanied by the sound of his riding crop rhythmically swishing through the air, and 'metaphorically onto the public's collective behind'. These modern prayers were also accompanied by the primitive beat of a tom tom.

> This is how the world is
> The bladder of the swine
> Vermilion and cinnabar
> Cru cru cru
> The great art of the spirit
> Theosophia pneumatica
> poème bruitiste performed the first time by
> Richard Hülsenbeck Dada
> or if you want to, the other way around
> birribumbirribum the ox runs down the circulum

For a variety of the cabaret's performances Marcel Janco produced abstract primitive masks which reinforced the Dadaists' search for the fundamental elements of the imagination, language and sound. These masks, which recalled the Japanese or antique theatre masks, seemed to have their own in-built character and demanded from their wearers appropriate gesture and costume. 'Inspired by their Protean individuality', Ball writes, the group invented dance steps and music which would express the masks' essence. 'Flycatching', 'Cauchemar', 'Festive desperation', such were the names given to the resulting spectacles.

The teamwork of the group also resulted in the creation of simultaneous poetry, such as the well-known '*L'amiral cherche une maison à louer*' which was performed by Hülsenbeck, Janco and Tzara as a 'contrapuntal recitative' in which their voices simultaneously spoke, sang, whistled, and made noises, all in a variety of recognizable and unrecognizable languages. As Tzara was quick to point out, the *poème simultané* was a poetic recreation of what the Cubists had done in painting, and it permitted each listener to associate freely with whatever elements in the poem struck a chord for him.

The Cabaret Voltaire was forced to close its premises at the end of 1916. The good citizens of Zurich had begun their own protests and the police were far more inclined to believe that this suspiciously noisy international group was a bevy of spies, rather than the quiet, scholarly Herr Lenin, who lived across the street and spent his days in the public library. Dadaist activity continued, however, in the numerous exhibitions which introduced modernist art to Zurich and through a series of Dada evenings, akin to Cabaret Voltaire performances. The evenings were *Gesamtkunstwerke*, total art works, and included theory, manifestoes, dance, music, poems, pictures, and theatrical sketches, all bearing Dada's particular experimental stamp and insulting the audience either directly, or because it was puzzled by the nature of what was happening on stage. It was at one of these evenings that Hugo Ball gave the climactic performance of his Dada career.

Wearing a Cubist costume, designed by Janco and himself, Ball was literally encased in a 'tight-fitting cylindrical pillar of shiny blue cardboard which reached to my hips so that I looked like an obelisk. Above this I wore a huge cardboard coat collar, scarlet inside and gold outside, which was fastened at my neck in such a way that I could flap it like a pair of wings by moving my elbows. I also wore a high, cylindrical, blue-and-white-striped witch-doctor's hat.'

So dressed, Ball recited, then chanted the first abstract, phonetic poem:

gadji beri bimba glandridi laula lonni cadori
gadjama gramma berida bimbala glandri galassassa laulitalomini . . .

A storm broke in the audience and luckily Ball, who was immobilized by his costume, just managed to calm his hearers by proceeding to a liturgical crescendo. Then, bathed in perspiration, he was carried off the stage. Ball explained the reasoning behind abstract poetry in his diary.

The human figure is progressively disappearing from pictorial art, and no object is present except in fragmentary form. This is one more proof that the human countenance has become ugly and outworn, and that the things which surround us have become objects of revulsion. The next step is for poetry to discard language . . . In these phonetic poems we want to abandon a language ravaged and laid barren by journalism. We must return to the deepest alchemy of the Word, and leave even that behind us, in order to keep safe for poetry its holiest sanctuary.

On 9 April 1919 Zurich Dada held its final soirée. The format was much the same as on other evenings. But this time, despite an enormous uproar during the second act in which some members of the enraged audience went so far as to brandish a piece of the balustrade, the final part of the programme was accepted with relative calm. Metamorphosed into a mob, the audience had suddenly seen the face of its own irrationality. Dada's conscious use of unreason had provoked a momentary illumination. The evening's huge takings, together with the audience's final acceptance of the programme, signalled the end of Dada's 'live' impact. The avant-garde, like the cabaret, cannot outlast that shock effect, that dissent which gives it life. Dada was, however, to travel to new locations, take on new problems, and be given different shapes by other artists. The far-ranging possibilities which its radical negation of the past and its experimentation had opened in the domains of performance style, music, design, not to mention graphics, are too well documented to need attention here.

Paris Dada

Post-war Paris was a city which, unlike Zurich, had a history of avant-garde antics and artistic scandals. But nothing yet could match the sheer tumult which the Dada 'happenings' produced. Lacking a cabaret 'base', the Paris Dadaists staged a series of vociferous stunts, soirées and congresses in which they savagely proclaimed that Art with a capital A was dead. The insane barbarism of the war had left culture and society in ruins and Dada was there to shout an 'inventory' of the fossils in a disaster area.

Tristan Tzara arrived from Zurich to become the questionable leader, but acclaimed publicity chief, of the movement. A group of Paris Dadaists, who had contributed to Zurich Dada, were already gathered round the magazine *Littérature* – André Breton, Louis Aragon, and Philippe Soupault. Francis Picabia, another participant in the Zurich days, was providing the Paris public with examples of Dada in his journal *391*. It needed only Tzara's exhibitionistic gift to draw Paris into the vortex of Dada. And despite the fact that the Paris movement functioned outside a 'cabaret', it maintained an insistence on the artists' personal performance in public, and on a variety of acts within a given *soirée*.

This post-war Dada reflected the nihilistic savagery, the incoherence which four years of bitter fighting had wrought. Dada was less wittily playful, more violently militant. Its rabidly anti-bourgeois slogans showed a growing political involvement with the working class, a tendency which was to become evident in the split within the movement some years later. Picabia's *Manifeste Cannibale Dada* read at the *soirée* of 7 March 1920, the twenty-fifth anniversary of the notorious première of Jarry's *Ubu Roi*, reveals these increasingly provocative tactics. 1200 spectators had been turned away from this gala event. People fought over seats. Some brought musical instruments to interrupt the proceedings.

You are all indicted; stand up! It is impossible to talk to you unless you are standing up; Stand up as you would for the *Marseillaise* or *God Save the King*.

Stand up, as if the Flag were before you. Or as if you were in the presence of Dada, which signifies Life, and which accuses you of loving everything out of snobbery if only it is expensive enough.

One dies a hero's death or an idiot's death – which comes to the same thing. The only word that has more than a day-to-day value is the word Death. You love death – the death of others.

Kill them! Let them die! Only money does not die; it only – goes away for a little while.

That is God! That is someone to respect: someone you can take seriously! Money is the *prie-Dieu* of entire families. Money for ever! Long live money! The man who has money is a man of honour.

Honour can be bought and sold like the arse. The arse, the arse, represents life like potato-chips, and all you who are serious-minded will smell worse than cow's shit.

82

Dada alone does not smell: it is nothing, nothing, nothing.

> It is like your hopes: nothing
> like your paradise: nothing
> like your idols: nothing
> like your heroes: nothing
> like your artists: nothing
> like your religions: nothing.

Hiss, shout, kick my teeth in, so what? I shall still tell you that you are half-wits. In three months my friends and I will be selling you our pictures for a few francs.

Up to this point the *soirée* at the Théâtre de l'Oeuvre had been as 'respectable' as any gala Dada event could warrant. The Dadaists had even managed to perform their own plays without too much audience intervention: Tzara's *La première aventure céleste de M. Antipyrine*, a verbal boxing match in which motionless actors, dressed in sacks or suitcases, played their parts on a stage suffused in an unearthly green light; Ribemont-Dessaignes' *Le serin muet*; Breton and Soupault's *S'il vous plaît*. But under the frontal attack of the *Manifeste Cannibale* the audience ran riot.

The fury of this particular evening however, was miniscule in comparison to the famous session at the huge Salle Gaveau some two months later. The *soirée* consisted, as always, of a variety of acts – poems, sketches, manifestoes – and included Soupault's *Le célèbre illusioniste* in which multi-coloured balloons, each bearing the name of a famous man, were released; as well as Tzara's twenty-man musical item, *The Vaseline Symphony*. All the Dadaists present wore funnels or tubes on their heads. Breton had a revolver on each of his temples. Eluard was dressed as a ballerina. And this time the audience too was well armed, with tomatoes, eggs, even escalopes and beef-steaks. All these were projected at the players. The Paris audience had learned to take part in Dada's universal anti. An eye-witness, Madame Gleizes, gives the following account of a Dada evening:

Holding hands and forming a chain, like little girls in a round-dance, a dozen disillusioned young men (and there was certainly plenty to be disillusioned about) would move to the front of the stage and groan: 'No art, no literature, no politics, no republic, no royalists, no philosophers, no nothing – Dada, Dada, Dada.' . . . Just as in 1913, when they first heard the rumblings of *The Rite of Spring*, the enraged audience would shout, stamp, whistle. In the wings Tristan Tzara almost climbed the walls with joy: 'It's exactly like the Communist meetings in Berlin.'

The Paris Dada evenings were not all so uniformly dedicated to provocative sloganizing. Experimental music, including that of Les Six was played; designs by Delaunay and Van Doesburg and films by Man Ray were presented. An introductory exhibition of the work of Max Ernst was organized, accompanied by varieties of Dada buffoonery.

83

On the whole, however, the spirit of post-war Dada, like that of post-war cabaret, had gained a dimension of bitterness with its playfulness. The dour realities of the period served as a constant reminder that a revolution within art was not tantamount to social change. It was perhaps German artists who felt this most strongly.

Berlin Dada

The series of violent uprisings, strikes and mutinies which shook Germany in the last year of the war and in the period following the armistice of November 1918 demanded political involvement from artists. Ebert's majority Social Democrats, who constituted the Republic's first government after Kaiser Wilhelm had fled to Holland, all too quickly showed their right-wing tendencies and what was to be a continuing reliance on military and big-business power. There were revolutionary uprisings by the Spartacists in Berlin and by the Munich 'Reds', both of whom attempted to establish soviet republics composed of citizens' councils of workers, soldiers, and sailors. Ebert's Defence Minister, Noske, countered by unleashing the terror of the Freikorps, a right-wing militia which semi-secretly had backing in high military quarters. The savage street fighting in Berlin — 1200 dead in six days of Free Corps law — the brutal murders of leading revolutionary figures such as Rosa Luxemburg and Karl Liebknecht, the massacre of justice which this led to, are all well known. The Weimar Government was characterized by stumbling indecision. It was frightened of the left, and as a result relied on sources of power established in pre-republican days. Together with post-war inflation, mass unemployment, and mass hunger, these created the powder keg which was to explode into Nazism.

It was into this socio-political chaos that Dada stepped, allying itself with the revolutionary cause and shouting with the voice of its innate internationalism: 'Death to German culture'. Battling against that mental attitude which could accept and rationalize the carnage of war, Dada once again used its weapons of aggressive nonsense. Hülsenbeck, who returned to Berlin in 1917, later summarized the Dada position: 'For the first time in history the consequence had been drawn from the question "What is German Culture?" (Answer: "shit") and this culture is attacked with all the instruments of satire, bluff, irony and finally violence. Beyond anything else, Dada was the artist's revolver.'

German Dada drew into its circle some of the most important talents, each of whom took on his own playful Dada title. George Grosz, whose satirical drawings were already known, was known variously as Böff, Dadamarshal or Propagandada. Grosz had already appeared, face painted white and wearing dandyish clothes, in various cabaret-like evenings to recite anti-war poetry. At the first Berlin Dada *soirée*, he recited the following insult poem: 'You sons-of-bitches, materialists/bread-eaters, flesh-eaters-vegetarians!!/profes-

84

sors, butchers' apprentices, pimps!!/You Bums!!' Then he proceeded to relieve himself – in grotesque pantomime – in front of a Lovis Corinth canvas. The audience was enraged, and Grosz tried to calm them with the explanation that urine was an excellent varnish.

Among the other Dada members were Wieland Herzfelde, writer, organizer and creator of the left-wing Malik Verlag, who was known as Viz; and his brother John Heartfield, the inventor of photomontage, who was known as Mutt or Monteur-Dada. Then there was Dadasoph, Raoul Hausmann, artist, philosopher, poet and photomonteur; Oberdada, Johannes Baader, architect and madcap Dada publicist; and Walter Mehring, Pupidada, the main poet and cabaretist to emerge from the movement.

These figures created Berlin Dada for a brief moment, before separating off either into party politics or other artistic activities. Like the French, they staged Dada evenings and demonstrations in various parts of the city as well as outside it. They read simultaneous verse, created bruitist experiments and Dada-dances. In fewer than

Spartacist election poster calls on Communists to crush bourgeois parliamentarianism 1920.

85

thirty performances between 1918 and 1920 they laid the foundations for German anti-illusionist theatre of the twenties, influencing Piscator's Epic Theatre, the Communist Party's agit-prop revues, and the Bauhaus's Theatre Workshop.

They did more than this: they took 'theatre' out into the streets, for as Oberdada Baader declared, the world was their cabaret. 'Dada is the victory of comic Reason over the Demiurge. Dada is the cabaret of the world, just as the world is cabaret Dada. Dada is God, Spirit, Matter, and roast veal at the same time.' The Dadaists performed in the streets of Berlin. Grosz sported round the crowded Kurfürstendamm area wearing a death's head. Everywhere the Dadaists went, they shouted slogans and put up stickers with such sayings as: 'Dada kicks you in the behind and you like it.' In order to sell one of their activist periodicals *Jedermann sein eigner Fussball* (Everyman his own Football) – an expression which has become part of Berlinese, signifying contempt for authority and humbug – they formed a street procession, carrying gummed labels saying, 'Hurra Dada', which they stuck on the walls of police stations. The six-strong editorial board marched through both poor and sophisticated areas of Berlin acompanied by a small band playing sentimental airs. Crowds followed, and the periodical, which contained poetry by Mehring, illustrations by Grosz and Heartfield's photomontages, sold well. Mehring claims, it 'even looked like becoming a best-seller – and would have, if we had not been arrested on our way home from serenading the governmental offices in the Wilhelmstrasse.' *Jedermann* was banned, like previous agitational periodicals, and the group was charged with contempt of the armed forces and with distributing indecent publications.

The battle against authority by means of laughter and nonsense continued. On the inauguration day of the First German Republic, Oberdada Baader, standing in the gallery of the Weimar State Theatre, cast flysheets bearing the following statement in the direction of Weimar's major politicians:

Dadaists against Weimar
On Thursday 6 February 1919 at 7:30 p.m.
in the Kaisersaal des Rheingold (Bellevue-Strasse) the
OBERDADA
will be proclaimed as
PRESIDENT OF THE GLOBE . . .
We shall blow Weimar sky-high. Berlin is the place . . da . . . da . .
Nobody and nothing will be spared.
Turn out in masses!
The Dadaist Headquarters of World Revolution

The proclamation was signed by many of the leading Dadaists.

Among the acts which became standard in the Berlin Dada performances – audience insult aside – were Hülsenbeck's reading of his *Fantastic Prayers*; Grosz's and Mehring's 'Race Between the Sewing Machine and the Typewriter', presented as a boxing match contest, and their 'Private Conversation of Two Senile Men Behind a Fire-

Heartfield photomontage, *Jedermann sein eigener Füssball.*

George Grosz *Insider and Outsider* 1926 Carlo Ponti, Rome.

screen'; Gerhard Preiss's Dada mime dance, called 'Dada-Trott'; and Hausmann's reading of his 'Seelen-Automobil'. At the end of 1919, Erwin Piscator joined the Dadaists to create the first 'living' photomontage.

The climactic event of Berlin Dada was the First International Dada Fair held in 1920. It was a mixture of exhibition, carnival and political meeting. The tone of the fair was set by a large stuffed effigy of a German officer with a pig's head, which hung from the ceiling overlooking the proceedings. 'Hanged by the Revolution', read a large placard.

In the meantime, Kurt Schwitters, poet, writer and *Merzkünstler*, was holding his own Dada cabaret evenings in Hanover. Here he read from his humorous anti-romance poem about that loveable

87

Anti-Imperialist cartoon by Th. Th. Heine in *Simplicissimus*, 1911. The caption reads 'War and Cholera. Civilization makes its entry into Tripoli'.

character Anna Blume, and would experiment with those phonetic poems which were to become the *Urlaut Sonata*, a mammoth phonetic poem based on a sonata structure. Schwitters, as is evident in his *Small Story of the Revon Revolution*, fully believed that the origins of a socio-political revolution lay in an artistic revolution. An art based on laughter was for him the expression of a free, anti-authoritarian spirit – the dynamic foundation of a free people. The Nazi prohibition on humour was to prove his point and the Dadaists' by negation.

But the Dadaist's own cultural nihilism was itself an expression of the bankruptcy of post-war culture. For the majority of its members it constituted only a momentary position which was to be transformed into some kind of concrete political affiliation, or into an individualized aesthetic. In the Dadaists who brought their innovative talents from the 'cabaret of the world' to the intimate cabaret of the small stage, raucous negation was changed into a genuinely artistic critique of the social situation of the inter-war world.

90

The Roaring Twenties

Le Bœuf sur le toit

During the *belle époque* Paris had been the world capital of cabaret. In the twenties, strip club versions of the cabaret proliferated and Montmartre continued to have its chansonniers. These latter, however, seemed a little old-fashioned in this post-Dada era and it was only towards the turn of the decade, when such poets as Aragon began again to use the chanson form as a means of political protest, that the chansonnier became once more part of the cultural mainstream. During the central part of the twenties, it was clear that the innovative focus had shifted from verbal satire and presentation to experimentation in the plastic arts, the cinema and music. Paris was now above all the city of jazz, of the music hall, of the new sounds provided by Les Six, and of theatrical forms which, like Cocteau's concert-spectacle, *Le Bœuf sur le toit*, included dance, acrobatics, pantomime, orchestra, the spoken word and drama. Although such spectacles seemed to have assimilated both the circus and the cabaret, they were too large in scope for the cabaret stage to hold.

The epoch did, however, have one locale which, like the older Lapin Agile, functioned as a meeting place for artists and a centre for their improvisation. While the artists were of all kinds, the art in question was music. Musical experimentation and musical satire were the keynotes of the day, and the cabaret, an adaptable form, shifted with the times. These were marked by the discovery of American jazz.

On 10 January 1922 Le Bœuf sur le toit (the steer on the roof) opened its doors to the greatest of Paris artists and the glittering *beau monde*. To name only a few, Picasso, Braque, Tzara, Mistinguette, Brancusi, Ravel, Marie Laurencin, Darius Milhaud, Francis Poulenc, and, of course, Cocteau, the owner of the name if not of the actual locale, were present. It remained the centre of Paris night life for the next decade.

Le Bœuf sur le toit had grown out of a smaller bar, the Gaya, which Cocteau and Les Six had frequented because an American musician and fellow student of Milhaud's, Jean Wiener, played there. He played anything from ragtime to foxtrot to Bach brilliantly. The presence of Cocteau and his group drew so many people to the Gaya that the owner, Louis Moysès, decided to move to slightly larger quarters. So the Bœuf, most fashionable meeting place of the twenties, was born. Jean Wiener played with his partner, Clement Doucet;

Opposite
'Le Bœuf sur le toit' by Jean Cocteau.
Photo Harlingue-Viollet.

91

Above: The Berlin Dada Fair of June 1920 at the Burchard Gallery. *Left to right*: Raoul Hausmann, Hannah Höch (*sitting*), Burchard, Baader, Wieland and Margarete Herzfelde (*at back*), Otto Schmalhausen (Grosz's brother-in-law, sitting), Grosz and John Heartfield. *On the left*, Dix's War Cripples; *floating overhead*, the dummy that provoked a subsequent prosecution. From *The New Sobriety* by John Willett. **Below**: *War Cripples* by Otto Dix, a drypoint of 1920 relating to the big painting at the Berlin Dada Fair. Piccadilly Gallery, London, and Michael Hasenclever Gallery, Munich. **Opposite**: *Lovesick* by George Grosz, 1914. John L. Loeb Jr, New York.

black musicians dropped in or stayed; Artur Rubenstein, or indeed anyone giving a formal concert, would come in after hours to entertain and improvise. The sounds of Gershwin, Cole Porter, jazz and more traditional airs, would emerge from the Bœuf amidst incessant chatter. Picabia's painting of an enormous eye, 'L'Oeil Cacodylate', looked on over everything.

The standard American bar had come to Paris. Its music, jazz, was another popular form which the European artist would appropriate for his own purposes. And if Le Bœuf sur le toit was one of the mediums through which jazz was assimilated into the artistic avant-garde, then despite its peculiarities, the Bœuf emerges as a form of artistic cabaret. It was in Germany, however, that the cabaret form was to make its definite shape and emerge in the fullness of its satirical and artistic potential.

Berlin

In the tumultuous years which followed upon the armistice, Berlin, seat of the new Republican regime, emerged as Germany's first truly cosmopolitan centre. With the end of the stringent war effort and the relaxation of censorship, both moral and political, a new per-missive air pervaded the city. Gaiety bordering on hysteria was the keynote of the day. And for an all-too-brief moment, Berlin democrati-cally embraced all comers: expressionist artists and comintern agents, nudist dancers and sexologists, embezzlers and black marketeers, drug addicts, transvestites, pimps, courtesans, homosexuals, prophets vegetarian, magical and apocalyptic. The city became a harbour for a variety of Eastern European refugees: Russians fleeing the revolution, Balkan conspirators, Jews escaping Ukranian pogroms, Hungarians, Viennese, Poles.

The new cosmopolitan air was reflected in Berlin's blossoming news-paper and entertainments industry. No less than 120 papers – popular, highbrow, left- or right-wing – found their source here. Theatres sprang up overnight and cabarets mushroomed. These cabarets thrived on the death of censorship and the majority of them had little in common with the artistic cabaret so far described. The smoke and talk setting might be the same, but the intent was radically differ-ent: erotic entertainment for profiteers, speculators, and all those who could salvage a few marks from black market exchanges. The strip club, with a light covering of wit sometimes more, sometimes less elegant, was born. Cabaret journals with pornographic texts, drawings and photographs flourished, taking on such exalted titles as *Love in Art, Humour and Poetry; Gay Living – Cheerful pages for Literature, Art and the Stage . . . and other lovely things.* The sound of jazz rhythms, imported from America, pervaded the night air, and the city was caught up in an orgy of dance. The word *Amüsierkabarett* has been coined to describe these dives or entertainment cabarets (as differen-tiated from the Kabarett or artistic, satirical cabaret proper) in

94

which the beat of foxtrot, black bottom, and one-step throbbed. Erich Kästner catches the pulse of this frenzied, dancing Berlin, which pushed an almost desperate permissiveness into reaction, without catching its breath to reflect on 'liberation'.

> Here specialists can hardly say who's who
> Or tell the kidney from the heart.
> Here women are an all-male-crew.
> Here all men play the woman's part.

> Here young lads dance the latest hits
> At ease in gowns and rubber tits,
> While in falsetto they descant.
> Here women in tuxedos groan
> With Santa Claus-like baritone
> While lighting up – Havana brand.

> It's men who occupy the ladies' room here
> Putting powder gaily on their skin.
> No woman looks for bridegroom here
> Since each one's got a bride with whom to sin.

> Some here, from sheer wish to be perverted
> Found they had to the norm reverted.
> And if Dante had this place to visit
> He'd take poison just to miss it.

> No pig could find its way around this sty.
> What's true is false, what's fake is not,
> And everything is stewing in the pot,
> And pain's a laugh, and pleasure makes 'em cry,
> And up is down, and front's behind.
> Just shake your head – or lose your mind.

> For all I care – be your own self's concubine,
> Or if you like them strong 'n hairy
> Pick a mate from Barnum's bestiary.
> As far as I'm concerned – that's fine.

> Only stop the squealing that you're wicked,
> Mad and grand, because of where you stick it.
> All that traffic from behind
> Hasn't much improved your mind.
> That's that – for all your kind.

> 'Ragoût fin de siècle'
> (translated by Koka Koala)

Berlin's post-war permissiveness did not only produce a frenzied gaiety hovering over the surface of volcanic social problems, it also gave rise to a group of serious left-wing critics – intellectuals and artists – who chose to use popular forms, newspapers and journals, as well as the small cabaret stage, as the medium for exposing, satirizing, or evaluating the condition of German society. These men

transformed cabaret into an outpost of dissent, a finely tuned instrument for illuminating and battling contemporary ills. Satire was their weapon, those genres which personalize and give immediacy to an abstract or distant situation – the performed song, poem, or monologue – their means. They used them to pierce to the quick of that ulcer which was Germany.

Serious artists, these men succeeded in bridging that ever-widening gap, chronic in Western culture since 1800, between high or élitest art and consumer entertainment for a mass market. They thus fulfilled the objectives which the initiators of the German cabaret and chanson form had set down. However, the impact of a mass war and the enormity of its consequences meant that their battle went beyond that levelled against an ossified morality. These men became the self-appointed conscience of German social democracy. For a moment almost unique in Western history, artists conveyed a dream of a world where individual liberty, social equality and peace would prevail, in a mode of discourse common to everyone.

Kurt Tucholsky, Walter Mehring, Erich Kästner, Klabund, Joachim Ringelnatz, and tangentially Bertolt Brecht, were the leading lights. Their names ring familiarly to contemporaries of Weimar, but aside from Brecht, are almost unknown outside Germany.

Kurt Tucholsky (1890–1935)

Spiritual brother of Heinrich Heine, Kurt Tucholsky was the period's most influential satirist. Under four aliases, each with their distinct personalities, Tucholsky fought against the injustices and irreverently pointed out the inanities of Weimar Germany. As Erich Kästner put it, 'A little fat Berliner . . . tried to stop a catastrophe with his typewriter.' In so doing, he created not only chansons which were sung in all the best cabarets of Berlin, but also parodies, essays, aphorisms, fairy tales, and those famed babbling monologues of Herr Wendriner, that all-too-human personification of the Jewish Berlin businessman.

'Gay schizophrenia' was the description Tucholsky applied to his penchant for assuming different personalities for his various kinds of writings. Theobald Tiger, his jollity tinged by melancholy, was a cabaretist who wrote poems and songs, often set to his own music. Peter Panter, round and agile, responsibly assumed the task of dealing with literature, and created aphorisms – jibing, satirical 'Schnipsel', for which Tucholsky is rightly famous:

On account of bad weather, the German revolution took place in music.

The reader is fortunate: he can choose his own writer.

German Communist Party (KPD): A pity that you are not a Party member – so that you could now be expelled.

Kaspar Hauser was the slightly bewildered creator of thoughtful musings and narratives. The sour Ignaz Wrobel thrust angry barbs at the political and social situation; while Tucholsky occasionally emerged in person to deliver major political statements. The pseudonyms, like the man behind them, were well known, for Tucholsky's writings appeared regularly in a majority of Berlin papers and periodicals. But his name was most closely associated with *Die Weltbühne*, Germany's leading left-wing weekly, of which he was for some time an editor.

The story of *Die Weltbühne* is emblematic of the tragedy of Weimar Germany. Initially a theatre magazine, *Die Weltbühne* enlarged its scope after the war to become that singular entity: a journal which combined politics and culture. Its contributors were Germany's foremost left-wing intellectuals and they formed a critical team which exposed and fought the paper democracy of Weimar society. In a country where art, intellect and political involvement were generally held to be radically incompatible, the *Weltbühne* team attempted to bridge '*Macht und Geist*', political and intellectual power, a cause that Heinrich Mann continually championed. However, its mission to revolutionize the German burgher and worker, to present the rights and responsibilities which constitute democratic citizenship, and eradicate reactionary evils, was doomed to ineffectuality. The oncoming catastrophe could not be stopped with a typewriter.

Tucholsky was constantly haunted by the futility of his and the *Weltbühne*'s endeavours, despite the popularity of the weekly. He wrote in 1931: 'What worries me most is the problem of effectiveness. Does my work have any? (I don't mean success: that leaves me indifferent.) . . . I write and write – and what effect does it have on the conduct of my country?' In 1919, the *Weltbühne* circle was already being accused of the negativism of its criticism, its consistent attacks on the state of society and the nation, unredeemed by any constructive policy. Tucholsky's vehement reply in '*Wir Negativen*' (We Negative Ones), was marked by a love-hatred of Germany characteristic of his writings. How could *Die Weltbühne* be anything but ferociously critical, he asked, in a country where the revolution had failed; where the bourgeois was profoundly anti-democratic and extremist; where the politicians sole platform was the prosperity of the well-to-do; where the intellectual – whose influence on legislation was nil – could plan a revolution, proclaim that God was dead, propagate the most dangerous ideas, but always and only on paper!

'We cannot say "Yes". Not yet. We know only one thing: that we must sweep away with an iron broom all that is rotten in Germany. We will get nowhere if we wrap our heads in a black, white and red rag and whisper anxiously, "Later, my good fellow, later." . . . We want to fight with love and hatred.' Tucholsky called his Germans a people of judges and executioners (*Richter und Henker*), playing on the traditional 'A people of poets and thinkers' (*Ein Volk der Dichter und Denker*).

With the treacherous wisdom of hindsight, it is all too easy for us now to say that it was the very freedom provided by Weimar Germany

Opposite
Marx to Lenin when he reaches heaven: 'Little Father, Lenin, would you please finally tell Grandaddy Marx: what is actually meant by Marxism?' *Simplicissimus*, 1924.

99

which permitted *Die Weltbühne* to wield its critical assaults; and that the left-wing intellectuals' own inability to engage in direct political action facilitated the rise of Nazism. Tucholsky himself was plagued by such doubts. He always considered himself primarily a European rather than exclusively a German, and from 1924 on he absented himself for increasingly longer periods from Germany.

'In Europe a man is a citizen only once and a foreigner twenty-two times. The wise man, twenty-three times.' Tucholsky followed the wisdom of his own aphorism and earned criticism from friend and foe alike. France, the spiritual home of his satirical predecessors, Heine and the early cabaretists, represented for Tucholsky an enlightened urbanity beyond any Germany had attained. He spent much of his 'voluntary exile' there, as well as in Switzerland and Sweden, punctuating this with travels in Denmark and England. Throughout, however, his preoccupations were with Germany, as his many collections of writings prove. Among them *Deutschland, Deutschland über alles*, a photomontage book produced in collaboration with John Heartfield, remains possibily the most scathing denunciation of that philistinism, indifference and brutality which Tucholsky saw in the German character, qualities which he felt led directly to the catastrophe of Nazism.

Below right
Jacket by John Heartfield of *Deutschland, Deutschland über Alles* Kurt Tucholsky Archiv.

Below
Jacket for Tucholsky's *Learn to Laugh without Crying*. Kurt Tucholsky Archiv.

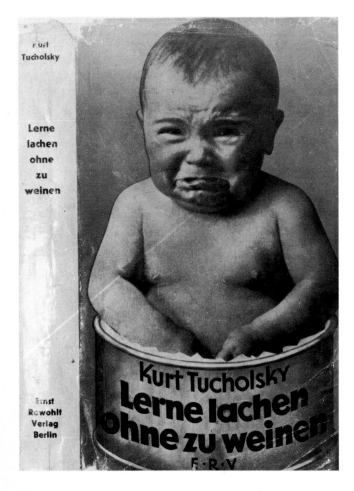

With the Nazi accession to power Tucholsky ceased to publish. Silence was the only path open to a man who had spent his life warning against the very events at hand. On the last page of his diary, he drew a diagrammatic ladder with three ascending steps: 'Speech – Writing – Silence'. Some two years after Hitler's triumph and the burning of Tucholsky's books Tucholsky's silence became total. In his Swedish home, he committed suicide by taking poison, a few weeks before his forty-sixth birthday. This final action was the first in a line of tragic suicides by German and Austrian literary figures. It spoke of utter exhaustion and of bitter disappointment. Germany's response to criticism had been to entrench those very evils which had been the focus of attack.

'Nothing is more difficult,' Tucholsky wrote, 'and nothing demands more character than to find oneself in open opposition to one's time and to say loudly: NO.'

He also wrote: 'Social poetry is no social revolution'.

His contradictions are still with us.

Walter Mehring (b.1896)

Walter Mehring was the most biting and verbally brilliant of the cabaret chansons writers. Son of a Berlin writer, the editor of the humorous magazine *Ulk*, and translator of French and American poetry, Mehring had an early education in the progressive values of the French Revolution and social democracy. His father had spent several months in jail at the turn of the century for his public criticism of Germany's reactionary regime, an episode which undoubtedly provided the four-year-old Walter with a deep suspicion of authority. His unconventional mother was an opera singer, and the household was constantly filled with the cream of Germany's artistic and intellectual life. Walter had no need of a better university and he terminated his formal studies with a high school diploma. At the age of fifteen he stumbled upon Marinetti and the Futurists' invocation to 'Destroy the museums. Crack syntax. Sabotage the adjective. Nothing but the verb . . .!' Mingling this poetically radical injunction with his illuminist heritage, Mehring produced songs and lyrics which capture the racy rhythms of modern city life and simultaneously evoke its absurdities, barbarities and injustices.

A youthful member of pre-war Expressionist circles, Mehring became one of the leading figures of Berlin Dada. He sang, recited and performed in a variety of locales: from army barracks to Spartacist meetings and Kurfürstendamm Kabaretts. This poem is an early specimen of Berlin Dada:

> *Hurra-r-r-r-r-a*
> *Tatü-Tata!*
> *Die deutsche Revolution!*
> *Schon naht*

Zylinderhut, Zylinderhut
Die Socialisierung
Oder das Auto im Stechschritt!
Schon revoltieren
Die ersten Lebensmittel der Entente
Im Magen der Kapitalisten!
Berlin, dein Tänzer ist der Tod – —[1]
Fortschritt und Jazz –
Die Republik amüsiert sich königlich –
Vergiss mein nicht zum ersten Mai . . .
(Dada-Prolog 1919)

Hurra-r-r-r-a
Tatü-Tata!
The German Revolution!
A top-hat, a top-hat
It appears already
Socialization
Or, the car in goose-step!
The first care-packages of the Entente
Already rebel
In the stomachs of the Capitalists!
Berlin: your dancing partner is Death – —[1]
Progress and Jazz –
The Republic entertains itself 'royally' –
Forget-me-nots for the first of May . . .

Mehring was the master of quick, earthy repartee, of Berlinese, that untranslatable dialect which mingled the savage wit of street talk, little man's humour and importations of foreign words. His chansons – which combined irreverently free associations, jazz tempos, and a big city language of slogans and hoarding advertisements – made him a popular success overnight. As his collection *Das Ketzerbrevier* (The Heretic's Breviary) published in 1921 makes clear, his work reflects the best aspects of the German post-war avant-garde.

Politically Mehring belonged to the same intellectual left as his friend, Tucholsky. A revolutionary pacifist, he was anti-bourgeois and championed the cause of the workers without ever strictly adhering to any political party. Like the other *Weltbühne* writers, he still believed in the power of verbal polemic: exploiters and exploitation could be fought by bringing people to consciousness of their situation as underdogs. Contemporary conditions could be radically changed by the force of illuminative reason and its weapon, satire. Furthermore, the engaged writer could function as a critic from within of the policies of the Social Democrats and of the left generally, and point out where those policies strayed from ultimate objectives.

One of the men who made up the 'conscience' of Weimar, a member of the 'negativists', Mehring, like Tucholsky, was by inclination and by choice an internationalist. From 1924 to 1928, he made his home in France, long regarded as a citadel of reason and wit by the German

[1] Slogan of a huge poster campaign launched by the government against strike action and Berlin's frenzy of amusement.

102

culture critic. His return to Berlin was marked by the production of his play, *The Merchant of Berlin*, by the important communist director, Erwin Piscator. The play created a scandal. Set in the inflation period, it tells the story of a rapacious Jewish merchant and makes dramatically clear the relationship between capital and militarism. Mehring was attacked not only by the rightist press for his exposé of the exploitative financial oligarchy and its link to the heavy arms industry; but by his friends for his alleged anti-semitism, since he linked profiteering with Jewishness. Like Tucholsky, Mehring was a Jew who was caught up in *Hassliebe*, love-hatred for his fellow Jews.

Mehring could be as critical of Communist Party tactics as he was of the state of bourgeois society. Though his sympathies and his analysis were always left-wing, he maintained a position of unaffiliated independence. In the last analysis, he placed more value on individual freedom than on party action. Tucholsky stated the basic problem for both of them and indeed, for many of *Die Weltbühne* circle: 'There is an organism called Man and everything hinges on him. And whether he is happy, that is the question. That he be free, that is the goal. Groups are something secondary – the state is secondary. The point is not that the state should live, but that Man should live.'

In 1930, during the Depression, Mehring was asked by the revolutionary proletarian newspaper *Die Linkskurve* to comment by what means the crisis which had shattered the economic life of the nations, and particularly of Germany, could be overcome. Mehring answered: 'Sir, am I a prophet? But I will divulge one thing: it won't turn out well! The religious thunder: "It will end with a divine ordeal!" The Nazis swear: "With the Third Reich." You want to hear: "With the World Revolution." Personally I see it this way. The capitalist system is collapsing, but this collapse will extend over a century and will be accompanied by wars, partial revolutions and technical and economic catastrophes. The first stage is the end of colonial serfdom.'

Despite his premonition that the rise of Nazism in Germany was inevitable, Mehring devoted all his energy and verbal wit from 1929 onwards to an acid attack on Fascism. In 1933 he fled to France and from there in 1940 to America, where like so many talented German exiles, he worked for a brief period in Hollywood. After the war, he settled in Switzerland and it was from here that he published his many monographs on art and his 'autobiography of a culture', *Die Verlorene Bibliothek*, the book which perhaps best illuminates the forces which shaped Germany's committed writers.

Klabund (1890–1928)

Among the many writers whose chansons were performed and who themselves appeared on the cabaret stage, Klabund alone emerges as an authentic *poète maudit*. Modelling himself on Villon, Klabund like Brecht, composed masterly ballads which sang the plight of the poor and the victimized. Born Alfred Henschke, Klabund's pseudonym seems itself to echo the spirit of his French predecessor, in its linking of 'Klabautermann', a ship's hobgoblin and 'vagabund'. His subtle lyrics first appeared in 1912 in the Expressionist magazine *Pan*, and they immediately earned him a prosecution for blasphemy. The romantic archetype stretches even further, for throughout his life, Klabund was plagued by recurring attacks of tuberculosis of which he finally died in the magic mountain sanatorium of Davos in 1928 – five years before the Nazis saw fit to burn his works.

A moral rather than a political radical, Klabund was initially caught up in the ringing patriotism which welcomed in the World War I. But the brutality of war experience quickly turned him to pacifism. Returning from Zurich in 1918 – where he had come into contact with the Dadaists – Klabund was thrust into jail by the authorities. His most acidly satirical chansons date from these early post-war years, when he was intimately linked with the cabaret and *Weltbühne* circles. But Klabund's most memorable work for the cabaret consists of finely accented poems in which his empathy for the downtrodden takes precedence over political satire. Here is one called '*Ich baumle mit de Beene*', a gem of Berlinese, which was set to music by Friedrich Holländer and sung by the urchin-like Blandine Ebinger. This translation by Dorothea Gotfurt transposes the scene from the backstreets of Berlin to London's Soho.

> Mum lies upstairs in the bedroom,
> Being in the family way.
> Sister Ann, who's got religion
> Goes to church where she will pray.
> I keep moping in the back-yard,
> Tearful and a little tense . . .
> And my legs are gently swaying
> While I'm sitting on the fence.
>
> Yesterday in Piccadilly
> I spoke with a real gent,
> One who has a Morris-Minor
> And a weekend place in Kent.
> Well, he offered me some lolly,
> Said his fortune was immense . . .,
> Cor! My legs are gently swaying
> While I'm sitting on the fence.
>
> Dad was caught when pinching bracelets,
> Now he's doing time once more.
> Nell, his slut went back to Soho,
> Mum is crying as before.
> Dad himself is not complaining –
> All this grumbling don't make sense . . .
> And his legs are gently swaying
> While he's sitting on the fence.
>
> Sometimes, when the moon is shining,
> I am crying out my heart.

When I'm thinking of me Charlie,
Who has robbed and killed a tart.
They will lead him to the gallows,
They will string him up and thence . . .
While his legs are gently swaying
I keep sitting on the fence.

Erich Kästner (1899–1974)

Erich Kästner, son of a Dresden master saddler, was already an established journalist when he arrived in Berlin in 1927, having been fired from his post on the *Neue Leipziger Zeitung* for publishing an erotic poem. He quickly became one of the *Weltbühne's* most popular contributors and indeed, with the publication of his volume of poetry *Herz auf Taille*, one of the time's most quoted poets.

In his 1928 collection, *Lärm im Spiegel*, Kästner coined the term *Gebrauchslyrik* for his kind of verse. The prose digression in this volume explains his use of the term and its intended attack on the obscurities of extravagant modernism and neo-romanticism.

There are poems from which even the literarily innocent person gets palpitations or bursts out laughing in an empty room. There are poets who feel like normal human beings, and express these feelings (and views and desires) by proxy. And because they do not write just for their own benefit and to show off their two-penny originality, they get across to people . . . Poets have their function again. Their occupation is once more a profession. They are probably not as indispensable as bakers and dentists; but only because rumbling stomachs and toothaches more obviously call for relief than non-physical ailments.

Gebrauchslyrik is a term which can be applied to all the topical, socially critical, humorous verse which made its way into the cabaret and its chansons. Witty, compassionate or caricatural, providing an immediately comprehensible analysis of social horrors, these were poems intended for everyone. Satire, Kästner stated, diagnoses the disease of the age . . . And the age demanded radical diagnosis.

Asked to write directly for the cabaret stage, Kästner rapidly emerged as a gifted inventor of chansons. These, along with his verses set to music, became staples of the cabaret and continued to be performed until 1934 – though under pseudonym in the last year. Kästner's work, like that of his fellows, was burnt by in Nazis in 1933, though Kästner was the only one of the twenty-three writers to be present at the gruesome ceremony. This world-famous author of *Emil and the Detectives* stayed in Germany throughout the Nazi period, despite the fact that his work remained unpublishable there. His reasons for remaining? A writer, Kästner stated, must experience how his nation acts in a time of adversity. It is his professional duty 'to take all risks in order to be an eye-witness and one day to be able to bear testimony.'

After the war, Kästner reengaged in cabaret work, writing for the *Schaubude* and the Munich-based, *Kleine Freiheit*. His work, which he called a mixture of 'accusation, elegy, satire, feuilleton, comment, caricature, frivolity, homily, lampoon and popular ballad' continues to be as topical today as it was in the era of its immediate 'functionality'.

Battling

What were the issues which these men, using all their critical ingenuity and verbal talent, confronted from the locus of the cabaret stage?

One of their primary concerns was to fight Germany's continuing militarism and glorification of war. After 1918 the nationalist propaganda machine fostered a 'stab-in-the-back' mentality. Germany was presented as the innocent victim of aggressive enemies who had launched a war out of envy for the Reich's growing power. (Any public questioning of Imperial Germany's Innocence was treated as treason-

Poster depicting the famous nationalist 'Stab-in-the Back' mystique, 1924.

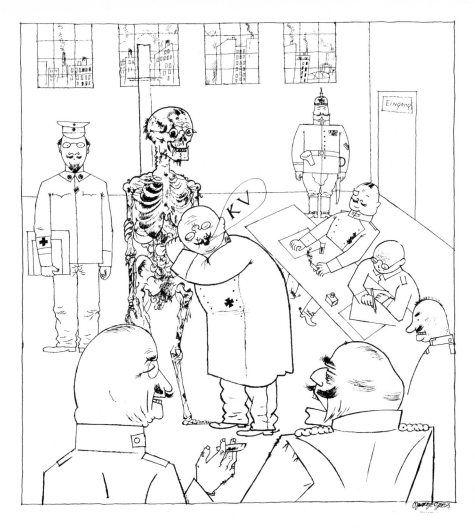

George Grosz, *The Faith Healers*, 1916–17. Museum of Modern Art, New York. A. Conger Goodyear Fund. The skeleton is pronounced fit for military service.

able and could result in a jail sentence.) Friedrich Ebert, First Chancellor of the Weimar Republic, himself propounded the myth that Germany's 'valiant armies had never been vanquished in the field'. Thus he left the path open for the immediate right-wing reaction that the Weimar Treaty was a sell-out, initiated by unpatriotic Social Democrats in collusion with the enemy. They had 'stabbed' the heroic German army in the back while it was successfully defending the Fatherland. Hitler, of course, was to make much of this remarkable piece of self-deception.

Revolutionary pacifists on the whole, the cabaret writers set themselves the task of deromanticizing war. They described the ordinary soldier's totally unheroic experience and pointed out that he was nothing but cannon fodder in a war which served big-business interests radically different from his own. In the macabre 'Legend of the Dead Soldier' Brecht uses the idiom of Nationalist rhetoric to expose the *real* value the authorities place on the individual's life. (George Grosz's *The Faith Healers* provides a similar comment on the exploitation and dehumanization of the common soldier.)

> And when the war reached its fifth spring
> with no hint of a pause for breath
> the soldier did the obvious thing
> and died a hero's death.

Poster for Max Weber's and Walter Rathenau's German Democratic Party's campaign against dictatorship by either left or right, 1920.

The war, it appeared, was far from done.
The Kaiser said, 'It's a crime.
To think my soldier's dead and gone
before the proper time.'

The summer spread over the makeshift graves.
The soldier lay ignored
until one night there came an official army medical board.

The board went out to the cemetery
with consecrated spade
and dug up what was left of him
and put him on parade.

The doctors sorted out what they'd found
and kept what they thought would serve
and made their report: 'He's physically sound.
He's simply lost his nerve.'

Straightway they took the soldier off.
The night was soft and warm.
You could tip your helmet back and see
the stars they see at home.

They filled him up with a fiery schnaps
to bring him back to life
then shoved two nurses into his arms
and his half-naked wife.

The soldier was stinking with decay
so a priest goes on before
to give him incense on his way
that he may stink no more.

In front the band with omm-pah-pah
intones a rousing march.
The soldier does like the handbook says
and flicks his legs from his arse.

Their arms about him, keeping pace
two kind first-aid men go
in case he falls in the shit on his face
for that would never do.

They paint his shroud with the black-white-red
of the old imperial flag
with so much colour it covers up
that bloody spattered rag.

Up front a gent in a morning suit
and stuffed-out shirt marched too:
a German determined to do his dut-
y as Germans always do.

So see them now as, oom-pah-pah
along the roads they go

and the soldier goes whirling along with them
like a flake in the driving snow.

The dogs cry out and the horses prance.
The rats squeal on the land.
They're damned if they're going to belong to France:
it's more than flesh can stand.

And when they pass through a village all
the women are moved to tears.
The party salutes; the moon shines full.
The whole lot give three cheers.

With oom-pah-pah and cheerio
and wife and dog and priest
and, among them all, the soldier himself
like some poor drunken beast.

And when they pass through a village perhaps
it happens he disappears
for such a crowd comes to join the chaps
with oompah and three cheers . . .

In all that dancing, yelling crowd
he disappears from view.
You can only see him from overhead
which only stars can do.

The stars won't always be up there.
The dawn is turning red.
But the soldier goes off to a hero's death
just like the handbook said.

(translated by John Willett)

This 'legend' earned Brecht a place on the Nazi black list as early as 1923, and in 1935 it was cited as the reason for his deprivation of German citizenship.

The deromanticization of war was not only aimed at past events. Writers of the left were also concerned with the Weimar government's growing dependence on the anti-democratic army and the militaristic fervour which continued to exist in nationalist sectors. Initially, the government's electoral platform had called for the democratization of the old Imperial army, as well as of the antiquated judiciary and civil service; socialization of certain industries, and a vast welfare scheme. Little of this programme was carried out. During the series of post-war insurgencies, the government, with Noske in charge of defence, turned increasingly to the army — which still maintained its core of Imperial officers — for help. Since the army could not totally depend on its war-worn rank and file, it semi-officially sanctioned the independent, anti-republican para-military organizations, the Free Corps, and a little later, the Black Reichswehr, who were all too ready to do away with 'unpatriotic' left rebels. Thus, though the Versailles Treaty stated that the German army could number no more than 96,000 men and 4,000 officers, and compulsory military service was abolished, by 1923 there were an additional fifty

Noske (left) and Ebert holidaying . . . while Germany crumbles. When this photo appeared in 1919 on the cover of the *Berliner Illustrierte Zeitung* it caused a sensation.

109

to eighty thousand men in the 'secret' reserve army, the Black Reichswehr. Germany was once more on the verge of being a nation run by its military and the pacifists were realistically adamant.

They saw the German people once again succumbing to that bogey of authoritarianism which precluded the development of democratic characteristics. Respect for a soldier-like discipline imposed from above and a mute kneeling to uniformed officialdom such as had marked Germany's Imperial regime, were a far easier task than assuming individual responsibility. Constantly, whatever the immediate matter at hand, Germany's left-wing intellectuals reiterated their critique of the 'good' burgher, or indeed the worker, who unquestioningly submitted to authoritative orders. In a bitter moment Lenin once said of the German revolutionaries that they would not even storm a railway station, unless they had first bought platform tickets. His statement proved all-too-true in the momentous year of 1919; but he might have added that with uniformed leadership which assumed a tone of total authority, not only the railway station, but all the cities it led to, might be effectively stormed.

In 'The Other Possibility', Erich Kästner ironically describes what Germany might have been like had the war been won; and simultaneously spoofs the authoritarian character and the nature of life under military nationalism.

If we had chanced to win the war
By dint of charging at the double,
Then Germany would be no more,
Would be a madhouse for its trouble.

They would attempt to make us tame
Like any other savage nation.
We'd jump aside if sergeants came
Our way and we'd spring to attention.

If we had chanced to win the war,
We'd be a proud and happy land.
In bed we'd soldier as before
While waiting for the next command.

Women would have to labour more.
One child per year. Or face arrest.
The state needs children for its store.
And human blood's what it likes best.

If we had chanced to win the war,
Then Heaven would be German national.
The parsons would be officers
And God would be a German general.

Then we'd have trenches for our borders.
No moon, insignia instead.
We'd have an Emperor issuing orders
And a helmet for a head.

If we had won, then everyone
Would be a soldier. An entire
Land would be run by goon and gun.
And round that lot would run barbed wire.

The children would be born by number,
For men are easy to procure.
And cannon alone without fodder
Are not enough to win a war.

Then reason would be kept in fetters.
And facing trial each single minute.
And wars would run like operettas.
If we had chanced to win the war —
But thank the Lord we did not win it!
(translated by Patrick Bridgwater)

The preponderence of the old Imperial guard, who clung, almost unchallenged, to their pre-war authority, in the top ranks of the military provoked some of Tucholsky's bitterest articles. Their anti-republican sentiments were well-known. Erich Ludendorff, leader of the Baltic Campaign, had supported the right-wing Kapp putsch, found wealthy industrial backers for it, and openly welcomed the putschists when they marched into Berlin. The coup was put down, not of course by the army, but by a general strike. When the untiringly conspiratorial Ludendorff then joined Hitler in his abortive Munich putsch, Tucholsky composed 'The Red Melody', possibly his most moving, certainly his most sung, political chanson. The voice is that of the mother of a dead soldier who warns Ludendorff that the people remember the horrors of war. Should he initiate this kind of disaster again, the people will unite with the ghosts of the dead to oust him from power. Set to music by Friedrich Holländer and sung by the inimitable Rosa Valetti, the song became one of the most inflammatory pieces of the epoch.

Ich bin allein.
Es sollt nicht sein.
Mein Sohn stand gegen die Russen.
Da fuhr man sie,
wie's liebe Vieh,
zur Front — in Omnibussen.
Und da- da blieb die Feldpost weg-
Haho! Er lag im Dreck.
Die Jahre, die Jahre,
sie gingen träg und stumm.
Die Haare, die Haare
sind grau vom Baltikum . . .
    General! General!
    Wag es nur nicht noch einmal!
    Es schrein die Toten!
    Denk an die Roten!

Sieh dich vor! Sieh dich vor!
Hör den brausend dumpfen Chor!
Wir rücken näher ran- Kanonenmann!
Vom Grab- Schieb ab-!

Ich sah durchs Land
im Weltenbrand —
da weinten tausend Frauen.
Der Mäher schnitt.
Sit litten mit
mit hunderttausend Grauen.
Und wozu Todesangst und Schreck?
Haho! Für einen Dreck!
Die Leiber — die Leiber-
Sie liegen in der Erd.
Wir Weiber — wir Weiber —
Wir sund nun nichts mehr wert . . .
                    (refrain)

In dunkler Nacht,
wenn keiner wacht —:
dann steigen aus dem Graben
der Füsilier,
der Musketier,
die keine Ruhe haben,
Das Totenbataillon entschwebt —
Haho! zu dem, der lebt.
Verschwommen, verschwommen
hörst du's im Windgebraus.
Sie kommen! Sie kommen!
und wehen um sein Haus . . .
        General! General!
        Wag es nur nicht noch einmal!
        Es schrein die Toten!
        Denk an die Roten!
        Sieh dich vor! Sieh dich vor!
        Hör den unterirdischen Chor!
        Wir rücken näher ran- du Knochenmann:—
        im Schritt
        Komm mit—.'

I am alone.
It shouldn't be.
My son has fought the Russians.
They drove them out
To the slaughterhouse,
They went to the front in buses.
And then and then the letters stopped.
Hi-ho! He lay in the mud.
And the years and the years
They went silently by,
And my hair and my hair

Has turned to grey,
As grey as the Baltic sea.
  General, general!
  Don't do it again, don't you dare.
  Hear the cries of the dead ones
  And think of the red ones.
  Take care! Take care! Take care!
  Hear the hollow sounding choir,
  We draw nearer, Canoneer!
  To the grave! Stay clear!

I saw the land
In the great war,
Saw thousand women crying.
The reaper was cutting
The women were suffering
A hundred thousand deaths.
And why this torture, why this fear?
Hi-ho, for nothing at all.
The bodies – the bodies
Are buried in the mud.
We women, we women
We don't count any more.
                        (refrain)

In the dark of night
When everyone sleeps
Out of the trenches they come.
The fusileer,
The musketeer,
who cannot rest in peace.
Battalions of the dead they soar
Up to the living hi-ho!
Hazily, faintly
You hear them in the storm.
They're coming, they're coming,
They're gloating round his home.
  General! General!
  Don't do it again, don't you dare.
  Hear the cries of the dead ones
  And think of the red ones.
  Take care! Take care! Take care!
  Hear the subterranean choir
  We draw nearer to the fire
  Death merchant! Here we come.
          (translated by Dorothea Gotfurt)

Social Democrat Election poster of 1924. Ludendorf is portrayed as a Nazi. The message: Wherever the General appears, men die by the hundreds.

It was officers like Ludendorff who sanctioned the brutality of the Free Corps and their murderous tactics towards the left wing. In the 'Casino Song of the Free Corps', Walter Mehring exposes the strutting barbarism of these forerunners of the SS.

113

Wir sind die Garde von der Spree,
Begehrt von allen Weibern,
Mit Achselstück und Portepée
Und wer'n die Stadt schon säubern.
   Tritt jefasst, die Augen links!
   Und die Bürger gaffen rings,
   Vorwärts marsch – und Beine streckt!
   Kriegt das Volk'n Mordrespekt,
   Ja, da staunen Sie,
   Wenn wir kommen, wie das fleckt,
   Bei uns'rer Kompagnie.

Wir schaffen Ordnung frohgemut
Und ohne Federlesen –
Und zahlt das Volk mit seinem Blut –
Der Bürger zahlt die Spesen.
   Wenn die Kerls auch rebellier'n –
   Nur nicht gleich den Kopf verlier'n!
   Feste druff, wo sich was regt,
   Bis sich keine Hand bewegt!
   Ja, da staunen Sie,
   Wie die Strasse reingefegt
   Von unsrer Kompagnie . . .

We are the guard of the River Spree,
Desired by women up and down,
With epaulette and porte-epée
We'll soon clean up this town.
   Ready march, eyes left!
   Burghers gape, you bet!
   Forward march, legs outstretched!
   Puts the People in mortal respect.
   When we come, the streets are made bloody
   By our company.

We create order with a smile,
And without much ado or fuss –
And if the People pay in blood –
Then the Burgher pays the expenses.
   And should the churls rebel –
   Don't lose your heads, by hell!
   When somethings stirs, pounce quick,
   Till not a hand can twitch!
   Yup, then they stare,
   When the streets have been wiped clean
   By our team.

A few years later, Germany's para-military thugs had found their emblem and their leader. In 1924 Mehring composed the *Lied der Hakenkreuzler"* or Swastiker's Song which exposes the 'hates' as

---

¹ 'Frisch, fromm, frölich und frei' was the slogan of the German Youth Gymnastics League, a nationalist and paramilitary organization.

114

The Aryan cult of the he-man mocked by *Jugend*'s Herbert Marxen. 'A healthy body houses a healthy mind — but sometimes only a very small one', 1931.

well as the tactics of the Nazis. Its marching rhythm echoes over two tragic decades of German history.

Links rechts links rechts
Kennt ihr diese Töne?
Links rechts links rechts
Für die Judensöhne
– Links rechts links Rechts – schaufeln wir das Grab
Hütet euch ihr Roten
Zählt euch an den Toten
Euer Schiksal ab!
Denn eine Uniform
Die imponiert enorm
Vor der gibt's keinen Sozialismus mehr –
Lasst das Proletenschwein
Nach Brot und Frieden schrein
Wenn das Signal kommt, rennt die Bande hinterher!

Links rechts links rechts
Lasst die Spiesser gaffen
Links rechts links rechts
Unser sind die waffen
Links rechts links rechts schwarzweissrotes Band

Lasst die Spiesser plärren
Wir sind eure Herren
Und das Vaterland
Denn unsre Schlachtmusik
Fegt eure Republik
Mit einem Ruck, mit einem Zuck bis in den Dreck
Das ist euch eingedrillt
Und wer nicht gut gewillt
Wird abgekillt und wir marschieren drüber weg
In den frisch-fromm-fröhlichen nächsten Krieg
Und wir sorgen, das ihr allesamt dabei seid
Wenn das ganze Volk auf der Strecke liegt
Leuchtet blutig uns das Morgenrot der Freiheit.

Left right, left right
Do you recognize these sounds?
Left right, left right
Meant to frighten Jewish sows
– Left right, left right – we shovel the grave
Beware all you Reds
Count off your fate
By the numbers of your dead!
For a uniform
Is enormously imposing
Socialism can't withstand it –
Let those pigs of proles
Shout for peace and rolls,
When the signal comes, the whole gang runs behind us!

Left right, left right
Let the Babbits look aghast
Left right, left right
Ours are the weapons to blast.
Left right, left right – black white and red band
Let Babbits babble ever faster
We are your only masters
And we – the Fatherland.
And our battle music
Sweeps your Republic
With a push and a pull into the dust.
Into you that's all drilled
And who isn't of good will
Will be killed – and we'll march over the dead
Into the happy and holy next war
And we'll take care that you're all there
When the body count's taken on the square.
Freedom dawns bloodily for us.

Because they felt threatened by the workers' uprisings and by the militancy of the revolutionary left, the Social Democrats had, from the moment they formed a government, played into the hands of the extremist anti-Republican right. In 1919, Noske issued an order to his troops which was to distort the face of Weimar justice for its entire life-time. The troops, he proclaimed, were to shoot if attacked or threatened with attack. Moreoever, they were to shoot if a prisoner were to escape, or even attempt to escape. Never, he added, can a soldier 'be excused for not doing his duty, if he fails to make use of his arms as prescribed by army law'. This was tantamount to sanction for wholesale slaughter. It also virtually gave the military power to determine what activities constituted treason. The result was that under General von Seekt, the Black Reichswehr reinstituted secret military tribunals, or *Femegerichte*, which dealt out summary justice to 'traitors'. The series of murders committed by these kangaroo courts, and the official military involvement in them, were exposed in the pages of *Die Weltbühne* during 1925.

But the entire nature of 'official' justice in Weimar was a matter of constant concern to the left-wing intellectuals. Throughout the pages of the left-wing press and the songs and writings of the cabaretists, one finds a critique of the reactionary 'state within a state' which Weimar judiciary constituted. The protest was aimed against the overt discrimination practised in the courts. Only a minute fraction of Weimar's judges were supporters of the Republic. As Lion Feuchtwanger reveals in his novel, *Success*, and as *Die Weltbühne* statistically demonstrated, justice in Weimar was essentially a right-wing affair. In the first four years of the Republic the courts convicted thirty-eight leftist offenders accused of twenty-two political crimes. Ten of these were executed, the rest given average sentences of fifteen years. The same period saw 453 rightest political murders. Twenty-three of the confessed murderers were acquitted. Only twenty-four of the offenders were convicted, but none were executed and prison sentences averaged four months. These murders were all seen as patriotic acts. When Count Arco Valley, the assassin of Kurt Eisner, Bavaria's Socialist president, faced a capital murder charge early in 1920, the public prosecutor stated: 'If the whole of German youth were imbued with such a glowing enthusiasm, we could face the future with confidence.' Arco Valley's death sentence was immediately commuted to life imprisonment, of which he served only a few years in a semi-open prison, prior to his release in 1924. Of Landauer's murderers, one was sentenced to a fine of five-hundred marks, while his military inferior received five weeks in jail. These typical travesties of justice sanctioned nationalist terror.

Not only did the political affiliation of the defendent, the prosecutor or the victim of murder, play a large role in the kind of justice meted out: the class designation of those who appeared 'before the law' in criminal or civil proceedings was of equal importance. One law for the rich, another for the poor, is not too simplistic an adage to apply to the majority of Weimar's discriminatory judicial proceedings. Thus widows or orphans of murdered workers were consistently deprived of even the smallest pension by the courts. The full severity of the anti-abortion laws was inflicted upon those who could not afford expensive 'secret' abortions. The long list of deplorable social conditions which may have led people to crime were never recognized

Weimar Justice as seen by *Simplicissimus*. The judge politely asks the right-wing assassin implicated in the Rathenau trial whether he sincerely felt called upon so young to play such a part in world history. The accused answers 'Why not? I always got B's in history'.

117

by the courts as a cause for lighter sentences. Many of the ballads of the period, which depict the plight of those forced into crime by harsh social circumstances, were directed against this simulated justice and were an attempt to elicit public understanding for the victim. Brecht's ballad of the infanticide, Marie Farrar, is a case in point. It tells the tale of a young orphaned girl whose various and bloody attempts at paid abortion fail. Miserably poor, she coldly murders the infant, having delivered it herself. She confesses her crime and is sentenced to a penitentiary. Brecht's refrain: 'You sirs, I beg, do not give way to indignation/Each creature needs the help of all creation' might serve as a plea to Weimar's judges who expected all those who came before them to act, think, and indeed speak in the accents of their own class code. As Tucholsky forthrightly stated, 'There is no such thing as an unpolitical criminal proceeding.'

In 'The Condemned Man has the Last Word', Mehring turns the tables on the society's entire understanding of justice. His condemned man has murdered a postal clerk and led a young virgin astray, but he still claims to be a moralist. Why? Well, it is only because criminals like him exist that lawyers and judges can go on earning a fine living. And finally, as the last stanza points out, his crime had been infinitely smaller than those perpetrated by the powers that be.

> An meinem Leichnam soll die Welt gesunden!
> Ich habe stets nur alles halb gemacht!
> Ich habe auch das Pulver nicht erfunden!
> Ich habe keinen Weltkrieg je entfacht!
> Das Morden ist die Kunst der grossen Geister,
> Die sterben hochgeehrt vom Vaterland!
> Kopf ab vor Euch! Ihr seid die wahren Meister!
> Mein letztes Wort: Ich war nur Dilettant!

> Will the world be improved by my corpse
> I only did things by half, no more!
> I did not invent gunpowder!
> I didn't kindle a world war!
> Murder is the art of great spirits,
> Who die respected by Fatherland!
> Hats off to you, you the true masters!
> My last word – I was a dilettante!

The hypocrisy of Weimar justice, or indeed any state justice, stands condemned.

In the cabaret literature of the period, the protest against the Weimar government's sanctioning of military power and general leniency to reactionary justice is connected with a satirical critique of grass-roots nationalism. This nationalism, fed by post-war cries of 'revenge on the Reich's aggressive enemies', received further fuel from the French occupation of the Ruhr in 1923 when Germany consistently refused to meet war reparations. It culminated in the Aryan myth of the fascists and their hate-mongering tactics. Humour was one of the few weapons which could be wielded against the irrationality of the basic nationalist position. The cabaretists used it to point out the foolishness of such a position; and also to demonstrate how nationalist fervour was manipulated into existence so that ruling interests might be served.

Tucholsky, chief amongst the internationalists, was a master of the anti-national joke. His satire was democratic and levelled at all the world's 'nationalities'.

The Danes are stingier than the Italians. Spanish women indulge in illicit love more readily than German women. All Latvians are thieves. Bulgarians stink. Romanians are braver than Frenchmen. Russians embezzle money.

None of these may be true – but you will see it in print in the next war.

This continent is proud of itself and has a right to be. What they are proud of in Europe: Of being a German. Of being a Frenchman. Of being an Englishman. Of not being a German. Of not being a Frenchman. Of not being an Englishman.

Once the nations organized a competition as to who could see the farthest. The Frenchman saw as far as the next Arondissement. The Englishman surveyed the whole world; it reflected him. The Berliner looked from the Kurfürstendamm past the Spree as far as the Alexanderplatz and thought that in between these lay America and the Atlantic Ocean. The Viennese didn't even bother to look; he was reading about a wonderful libel suit in his newspaper.

The fact that Germany's nationalism was fostered by the desperate conditions of everyday life in the post-war period needs no re-emphasis. The disastrous rate of inflation meant that the savings of the middle class were wiped out and a worker's salary was worthless by the time it was received. While in 1918 a loaf of bread had cost 0.63 marks, in November 1923 it cost 201 billion marks. A pound of butter cost the equivalent of two days' work for a skilled labourer; a suit of clothes, twenty weeks' wages. And this was if work could be obtained. Poverty was rife; money literally not worth the paper it was printed on.

Right-wing propagandists blamed this state of affairs on the very nature of republican democracy, on the allies, and on the Jews. True, the Weimar government did half-coincidentally profit by the inflation, since it managed to pay off its huge debt in 'paper money'. But the greatest profiteers, as the left commented, were the giant indus-trialists, whose expansionist needs had initially sent Germany into an aggressive war. They speculated against the mark, bought property, materials, labour, at what were apparently 'normal' prices, but did not settle accounts until the named sum had radically decreased in value. Thus they acquired huge empires. Most notorious of these speculators was Hugo Stinnes, whose property included coal mines,

The Demon of inflation will be burnt by us, promises the German Democratic Party. 1924.

Gegen eine neue Inflation für Reichseinheit und Republik für Loslösung von unseren Feinden

II/30

Rettung bringt die D.D.P.

Wählt Deutsch-Demokratisch

steel works, chemical factories, paper mills, newspapers, hotels and shipping lines. Hated by all those who opposed monopoly capital, Stinnes was the butt of much Weimar satire. While they were collaborating in the Munich political revue, 'This Far and No Further', Mehring, Heinrich Mann and Siegfried Vegesack wrote this song about Stinnes:

120

Hugo, wo hast du wieder deine Finger drin?
Hugo, wo schaust du Wieder mal so gierig hin?
Alle deine Taschen sind voll bis an den Rand
und du streckst nach überall die gierige Hand.
Kohle! Stahl! Papier! Alles ist schon dein,
Und du steckst dir immer neue Sachen ein!

Ich tu's ja nicht nur wegen des Gewinnes!
Ich tu's ja nur als grosser Patriot!
Ich bin ja nur der Hugo Stinnes,
Nur Stinnes, nur Stinnes!
Friss (oder Stirb!) mein Brot!

Hugo, what pie is your finger in now?
Hugo, where are you looking so greedily now?
All your pockets are full to the top
And still you stretch your paw without stop.
Coal! Steel! Paper! All already in your ken.
And you constantly stuff new things in.

I don't do it only for profit!
Patriotism's my real motive!
I'm only Hugo Stinnes,
Only Stinnes, only Stinnes!
Eat my bread, or die!

Speculation was possibly one of the few areas Stinnes did not monopolize single-handly. It was rife. Fortunes were made overnight and lost or spent as quickly in Berlin's numerous night spots, gambling clubs and cabarets, only to be remade. The country was caught in that speculation fever which Mehring's 'Song of the Stock Market' recreates:

Es braust ein Ruf wie Donnerhall:
Spekulieren! Spekulieren!
Es fuchteln Hände überall,
Den Kurs zu dirigieren ...

Es klingt durch den Verzweiflung noch,
Mag der Börsianer toben:
O Dollarkurs, wer hat so hoch
Dich aufgebaut da droben!

Gehts auf und ab in dem Gewühl
Gewinnen und Verlieren,
Uns eint doch alle ein Gefühl:
Spekulieren! Spekulieren!

Hear it roaring through the nation
Speculation, speculation!
Hands shoot up and men despair
Speculation everywhere.

In the general desperation
One thought penetrates the nation:

Why does the dollar, why oh why —
Climb up right into the sky?

Despondency and desperation
Are now sweeping through the nation
In the grip of the inflation.
What keeps them going? Speculation!
Speculation, speculation!

(translated by Dorothea Gotfurt)

The frenzied elation of the profiteers was in strong contrast to the plight of the workers. Those who had wealth might gain more and revel in the pleasures which the Kurfürstendamm offered, forgetting the millions who weren't present, as Klabund reveals in one of the best songs of the epoch:

Am Kurfürstendamm, da hocken zusamm'
Die Leute von heute mit grossem Tamtam.
Brillanten mit Tanten, ein Frack mit was drin.
Ein Nerzpelz, ein Steinherz, ein Doppelkinn.
Perlen perlen, es perlt der Champagner.
Kokotten spotten: wer will, der kann ja
Fünf Braune für mich auf das Tischtuch zählen ...
Na, Schieber, mein Lieber? – Nee, uns kann's nich fehlen,
Und wenn Millionen vor Hunger krepieren:
Wir woll'n uns mal wieder amüsieren ...

Die deutsche Revolution ist tot ...
Der weisse Schnee färbt sich blutigrot ...
Die Gaslaternen flackern und stieren ...
Wir woll'n uns mal wieder amüsieren ...

The now generation on the Kurfürstendamm
Flock together with a loud Tamtam.
The flashy with aunty, tail-coat with something in't.
Mink stole, heart of stone, double chin.
Pearls, pearls, it sparkles champagne.
Coquettes taunt; whoever wants it can
Pay five grand down on the table for me
Eh profiteer, my dear? No, nothing lack we.
And what if millions starve without a bun?
Once again, we want to have fun ...

The German revolution is dead
The white snow painted bloody red.
The street lamps flicker and stun
Once again, we want to have fun.

Mehring's less subtly poetical 'Dry Bread Song' provides a succinct activist analysis of the state of labour in a market economy. Performed in cabarets, it was also sung to Hans Eisler's music in the political revues attended by working-class audiences.

122

Wer arbeit'muss auch essen. Und weil er essen muss
Das macht das Essen so teuer – dass er mehr arbeiten muss
Und wenn er noch mehr arbeit't – is mit der Arbeit Schluss
Dann gibt es keine Arbeit – so dass er hungern muss!

Rechten Linken! Rechten Linken!
Trocken Brot und Wasser trinken
Das ist unsere Welt!

Wer hungert, kann nich arbeit'n Wer nich arbeit't braucht kein Brot
Brot gibt's nich ohne Arbeit – kein Brot is Hungersnot!
Und Hungern, das tut Wunder – das ist eine Himmelsmacht
Daran haben sich Millionen – Millionen gesund gemacht . . .

He who works must also eat. And because he must eat,
That makes food so dear, he has to work till he's beat.
And if he works even more, well that's the end of the show.
For then there's no more work, and he must hungry go!

Right and left! White and Red!
Water to drink and dry bread.
That's our world.

The hungry cannot work. No work, no need for bread.
No bread without work – no bread, you're dead.
But going hungry does wonders for one – it's a heavenly might!
By it millions, yes millions, have made themselves healthy, all right!

But it is perhaps Tucholsky's song, 'Shopping 1919', which best captures the tone of the post-war satirical cabaret. Lightly lyrical, playfully hiding behind a good-humoured naivety, it juxtaposes the prevailing attitudes in Germany with the issues for which the cabaret-ists fought until the Nazi regime brutally stilled their voices: either blindly patriotic nationalism or an objective analysis of the war, either massacre, the forces of right-wing reaction, or a truly democratic

Trude Hesterberg singing Walter Mehring's 'Song of the Stock Exchange'. Courtesy Walter Mehring.

republic. The 'Michel' here in question is the traditional figure of that little boy who represents all of Germany.

Was schenke ich dem kleinen Michel
zu diesem kalten Weihnachtsfest?
Den Kullerball? Den Sabberpichel?
Ein Gummikissen, das nicht nässt?
 Ein kleines Seifensiederlicht?
 Das hat er noch nicht. Das hat er noch nicht!

Wähl ich den Wiederaufbaukasten?
Schenk ich ihn noch mehr Schreibpapier?
Ein Ding mit schwarzweissroten Tasten;
ein patriotisches Klavier?
 Ein objectives Kriegsgericht?
 Das hat er noch nicht. Das hat er noch nicht!

Schenk ich den Nachttopf ihm auf Rollen?
Schenk ich ein Moratorium?
Ein Sparschwein, kugelig geschwollen?
Ein Puppenkrematorium?
 Ein neues, gescheites Reichsgesicht?
 Das hat er noch nicht. Das hat er noch nicht!

Ach, liebe Basen, Onkels, Tanten –
Schenkt ihr was. Ich find es kaum.
Ihr seid die Fixen und Gewandten,
hängt ihr's ihm untern Tannenbaum.
 Doch schenkt ihm keine Reaktion!
 Die hat er schon. Die hat er schon!

What shall I give little Michel
For this cold Christmas feast?
A bouncing ball? A drooler's bib?
A small light next to his crib?
 A rubber cushion? Never gets wet.
 He hasn't got that yet.

Shall I choose a reconstruction kit?
Perhaps more writing paper?
A thing with black, white and red keys;
A patriotic piano?
 An objective war tribunal?
 He doesn't get that as a rule!

Shall I give him a bedpan on wheels?
Or offer him a moratorium?
A roundly swollen piggy bank?
Or perhaps a doll's crematorium.
 A new intelligent face for the nation?
 That would fill him with elation.

Oh dear cousins, uncles and aunts,
Give him something. I don't know what it might be.
You're the quick and clever ones,

124

Hang it for him on his Christmas tree.
　　　But please don't give him reaction
　　　He's already had that to distraction!

Simplicissimus' view of Christmas 1919.

Whether the cabaretists' satirical weapons had any impact upon the affairs of the nation is impossible to ascertain statistically. Certainly though, satire had some unmeasurable effect upon the consciousness of the people, if only by undermining prejudices and received beliefs –

125

or so Hitler's dictatorship proved by negation. Cabaret writers numbered among the first victims of the Nazi terror. Indeed, the Nazis' chief anti-semitic publicist, Julius Streicher, pleaded the ultimate case for the efficacy, indeed necessity, of the cabaret spirit and of laughter and satire generally, when he declaimed in Nuremberg in 1938 against a still existing and comparatively mild cabaret: 'Should there dare to be once more in this town of the party conventions, such prattle and jokes directed against a political leader, then we shall close down the cabaret the *Bude*. I shall cut down every such conférencier . . .'[1] The intellectuals want this kind of mockery. They mocked everything that was respectable. It is however impossible to maintain a State, which as an organization serves the people, when every stupid young upstart can mock at it.'

But the greatest irony lies in the fact that a mad upstart had already taken the nation over.

Sekt, smoke, sex, and satire

A heady mixture of sekt and smoke, jazz and pornography, song, sport and stinging satire – such was the post-war Kabarett. Its seductive atmosphere, at once sentimental and erotic, finds its most authentic record in Josef von Sternberg's 1929 film classic, *The Blue Angel*. Loosely based on Heinrich Mann's novel *Professor Unrath*, the film brought together some of the greatest cabaret talent – the actor-singer, Kurt Gerron, the dynamic *diseuse*, Rosa Valetti, the composer Friedrich Holländer – and introduced to an international public a woman who was to incapsulate the entire myth of femininity for the roaring twenties: Lola-Lola, alias Marlene Dietrich. Ironically enough, Dietrich was the least known of the personalities appearing in the film. Sternberg spotted her doing a bit part in a revue and asked her to audition and . . . The rest of the tale has become public history.

The film portrays a petty-tyrant school-teacher (Emil Jannings) who learns that his students frequent a kind of 'Amüsierkabarett', the Blue Angel, where the star attraction is Lola-Lola. Outraged the professor decides to confront the vicious siren who has been corrupting the morals of his young pupils. Instead he falls victim to her tangible charms, proposes to her, and having been forced by conventional morality to leave his teaching post, tours with the artistes. Having demonstrated on his wedding night that he can do a marvellous imitation of a rooster, the professor is convinced by Lola-Lola – who renders him progressively more jealous with her insolent sexuality veiling a cool impassivity – to perform this mimic feat on stage. The troupe, sure of success with this clown act, travels back to the professor's home-town. Here, in a paralysis of abject humiliation, he launches into a terrifying 'cock-a-doodle-doo' before a large local

[1] The word Streicher uses rather than the more usual 'conférencier' is 'Ansager'. The Nazis had already begun their aryanization of the German language.

126

audience which contains some of his former pupils. Then, still crowing, he rushes off-stage to try to strangle Lola-Lola. He is stopped by the artistes, and put in a strait-jacket. When he awakes from his madness he recognizes the full horror of his situation. Like some large wounded animal, he stumbles towards the schoolhouse, where he was once master rather than subject, to die on familiar terrain while Lola-Lola sings on in the cabaret.

Plumbing the depths of that sado-masochism which was so tragically to mark Germany's collective psychic history, the film owed its international success as much to its unforgettable songs as to the charms of Lola-Lola, Emil Jannings's dramatic genius, and Sternberg's direction. This music was the product of Friedrich Holländer, one of the post-war Kabarett's greatest composers.

In his autobiography, named *Von Kopf bis Fuss* after one of the songs in the film, Holländer recounts how, tinkling away at the piano, he managed to compose the melody for his song, but was stuck midway through the second line for words. When Sternberg asked to hear it, Holländer played through the finished section, and shrugging added '*und sonst garnichts.*' and nothing else. These accidental words became one of the main motifs of the film, and the song haunts the professor's enthrallment, humiliation and death. It is the very emanation of Lola-Lola: its saucy, racy tones, cruelly mingle irresistible sexuality with impassive promiscuity.

> *Ich bin von Kopf bis Fuss auf Liebe eingestellt*
> *Denn das ist meine Welt und sonst garnichts.*
> *Das ist – was soll ich machen – meine Natur.*
> *Ich kann halt lieben nur und sonst garnichts.*
> *Männer umschwirren mich wie Motten um das Licht*
> *Und wenn sie verbrennen dafür kann ich nichts.*
> *Ich bin von Kopf bis Fuss auf Liebe eingestellt*
> *Denn das ist meine Welt und sonst garnichts.*

> From head to foot, I'm made for love
> For that is my world and nothing else.
> That is – what can I do – my nature.
> I can only love and nothing else.
> Men cluster round me like moths round a flame
> And if they burn, I'm not to blame.

Holländer's musical and dramatic talent had a family background. His father, Victor, was a well-known theatre composer; his uncle Gustav, a classical musician and founder of a conservatory; his uncle Felix, was Max Reinhardt's chief dramaturge. Friedrich himself could range from such provocative mood pieces as Lola-Lola's theme song to providing music for Tucholsky's and Mehring's most violent satirical chansons. From the cabaret stage he went on to produce satirical cabaret-revues, and from there to Hollywood, where he wrote the music for some 175 films – an output to rival Wagner's.

The more artistic and committed of the German post-war *Kabaret-*

ten were more akin in spirit to the totality of the film, *The Blue Angel*, with its bitter exposé of the German character, than they were to the actual stage sequences presented within the film. To the eroticism, sentimentality and variety of these, they added satire, protest, and the use of avant-garde techniques and materials. Indeed, in the early post-war years, the Kabarett was associated with the most radical artistic movements and experimenters. And these, in turn, found their art influenced by cabaret.

The Kabarett inherited some of its most skilled participants from the German Dada movement. It also took from it an extended definition both of the limits of art, and of the possibilities of protest and provocation. Anti-traditional, the cabaret had always understood 'art' and 'literature' to include a much wider spectrum of activities and products than were conventionally designated by these terms. Now, all cultural manifestations from the boxing match to the bicycle race[1] — the symbolic forms of popular struggle — became part of an artistic terrain which quickly extended to jazz and the American pop-song. Indeed, American imports — used half-satirically, half romantically — marked the whole era, as these transformations in name denote: Walt Merin, George Grosz, and John Heartfield who had already taken an English name in protest against German militarism during the war. While this conscious appropriation of American culture seems, at first glance, to be in contradiction with the professed left-wing sympathies of its champions, the dilemma can soon be resolved. In comparison to Germany a romanticized 'Wild West' America did have a genuinely popular culture, and the tendency of the German post-war avant-garde was to incorporate the popular into what was essentially an élitest artistic tradition.

This movement towards the popular was of course not an end in itself. It had a political and social orientation. By using popular forms, writers and artists could convey to a larger-than-ever number of people the reality of their contemporary situation and the necessity for social change. Towards the mid-twenties, this trend toward committed art coalesced around Neue Sachlichkeit, the New Objectivity movement. Reacting against the heroic and mystifying optimism of the Expressionists and their modernistic techniques, which were impenetrable to the ordinary man, the New Objectivists propagated an art which would deal realistically with the life of the ordinary individual in terms which were both comprehensible to him and entertaining. In film, drama, poetry, fiction and music, the stress was sociopolitical and satirical.

To be popular meant to be entertaining. As any one in show business will testify cynically or not, the formula for entertainment, spectacle aside, is a tang of eroticism, a touch of sentimentality, music with contemporary words, a strong rhythm, or a melody which can be whistled, and jokes, wit — anything that produces laughter. These are

[1] See, for example, Brecht's stage-metaphor of the wrestling ring in *In The Jungle of the Cities*; Kaiser's use of the cycle race in *From Morning to Midnight*; and in France, the avant-garde's birthplace, Jarry's *The Passion considered as an Uphill Bicycle Race*.

Brecht with clarinet next to Karl Valentin with tuba at the Munich Oktoberfest. Standing is Liesl Karlstadt. Courtesy Stadtarchiv, Munich.

the elements which, of course, in varying proportions make up the cabaret chanson and indeed the cabaret's entire programme. Linked with the fact that the impetus behind the cabaret's development had always been marked by protest, social commitment, insistence on the contemporary, and a move towards the popular, it is not surprising that German artists at this time chose to go to school to cabaret. They enriched it, and it, in turn, influenced their work. Because of the entertainment it provides, the cabaret is in many ways the perfect medium for an art which seeks to be popular.

It is interesting to note just how much the cabaret influenced Brecht and through him twentieth-century theatre. Brecht really belongs to the satirical New Objectivist tradition, a fact which often passes unnoticed. As early as 1924, he was speaking of an 'epic smoke theatre', a place where people might come casually, not hushed in awe, to watch and participate in a performance, either through discussion or interference. To Brecht a smoking audience seemed to imply a thinking audience. And as in cabaret, talk and drink could be another important part of the spectacle. In *The Baby Elephant*, one of the stage directions reads, 'The audience goes silently to the bar and orders cocktails'.

Brecht's theory of *Verfremdungseffekt* or the alienation effect, grows as much out of the cabaret stage and setting as it does out of the boxing ring and the popular music hall. All these forms break down the fictional distance between player and spectator. The actors play directly to their audience, not primarily to each other, and any feedback from the audience is incorporated into a spectacle which includes them both. In the same way Brecht's alienation effect demands that both audience and player are distanced from their habitual roles so that both can see around these. The actors constantly 'send-up' the illusion that reality lies in the on-stage fiction and that they *are* the characters they are portraying. Their insistence on the fact that they are merely playing a role which they can clearly see around, wakes the audience into an awareness of its own role as an audience. Brecht's use of a 'poor' stage almost bare of props and effects, reinforces this break down of illusion. It, too, parallels the generally 'poor'

130

stage of the cabaret performance. During his Danish exile, when large-scale productions of his work were almost impossible to manage, Brecht was forced to rely more and more on the small 'poor' stage – a necessity metamorphosed into one of the trademarks of his craft.

Brecht – like the anti-hero of his first play, *Baal* – began his career as a strolling balladeer. He performed in various locales, including cabarets around Munich. His delivery was devastating, as Lion Feuchtwanger, testifies in his novel *Success*, where Brecht appears as Kaspar Pröckl. This description of Brecht's early songs places him directly in the cabaret and New Objectivist tradition. 'Then he planted himself in the middle of the room and with open effrontery in a horribly loud shrill voice, began to deliver his ballads to the twanging of a banjo, pronouncing his words with an unmistakenly broad accent (the local Bavarian German). But the ballads dealt with everyday happenings in the life of the ordinary man from the point of view of the large town, and as they had never been seen before; the verses were light and malicious, spiced with impudence, carelessly full of character . . .'

In collaboration with Kurt Weill, the sentimental and satirical song became one of the main innovatory points of Brecht's drama. As he claimed, it was to the language of the popular cabaret song that he turned for a model, for it contained that essential quality of *Gestus*, that possibility of at once presenting attitude and gesture. The immediate success of *The Threepenny Opera* would partially be due, one would imagine, to its structural rudiments being already known in embryo form to the Berlin world.

The short, sketch-like scenes of the cabaret performance, which were non-consecutive but loosely linked through satirical and political intent, also left their mark on Brecht's work, as *Terrors and Misery of the Third Reich* and *The Resistable Rise of Arturo Ui* make clear. Finally, Brecht's use of a narrator who steps out of the fictional dramatic framework to comment on events within the play is reminiscent of the cabaret's voluble conférencier and his running monologue on acts and contemporary events. Many of Brecht's actors, it should be noted, came from the cabaret stage.

Not surprisingly, in 1922, several nights after the Munich première of his *Drums in the Night*, Brecht opened his own cabaret, Die Rote Zibebe, the Red Grape. A late-night show which began after the final curtain had come down on *Drums*, it took its name from the tavern where a scene of the play takes place. The tavern host, Blubb, became the cabaret's conférencier. His players emerged from beach-cabin-like boxes, when he drew each of their separate curtains, only to disappear into them again when their acts were over. Apart from Brecht himself, Die Rote Zibebe featured Klabund, Ringelnatz, the singer Annemarie Hase, the dancer Valeska Gert and the renowned Munich comic Karl Valentin. Unfortunately, Die Rote Zibebe did not have a long history. The police only granted the establishment a provisional licence, which was quickly withdrawn. Brecht was already in the authorities' bad books for his pronounced critique of war 'heroism'.

SCHALL UND RAUCH

Schall und Rauch

The first post-war literary cabaret opened its doors in December 1919. Max Reinhardt, director of Berlin's Grosse Schauspielhaus wanted, once again, to have parodies of his large-scale productions put on 'underground' in the basement of his converted circus. And so, the second Schall und Rauch, sound and smoke, was born, numbering among its collaborators Mehring, Tucholsky, Klabund, Holländer, and some of Germany's most talented performers. Sharply political and satirical, and left-wing in orientation, the cabaret set the tone for the witty critique of current affairs which was the mark of the period.

The main event of the opening programme was a parody of the *Orestia*, the current production on the Reinhardt stage. The cabaretists devised a puppet play entitled, *Simply Classical! An Orestia with a Happy Ending*. Mehring prepared the script. George Grosz designed the puppets. John Heartfield constructed the masks and the marionettes which were about two-foot high, with the help of Waldemar Hecker, the Eleven Executioners' puppet-maker. Friedrich Holländer wrote the music. This high-powered team produced a witty piece of contemporary political commentary. Agamemnon appeared as 'a general in his best years'. Aegisthus, 'a literary man and professional moralist' emerged as Ebert, the new democratic president. Clytemnestra appeared in the guise of a cabaret artist. Electra was a Salvation Army girl, since, as the avant-garde ironically claimed, this was the period's most 'mysterious' religion. The chorus was played by an alienating gramophone which kept interrupting the action with political songs. And Orestes was an officer of the Attic Free Corps. In the second half of the play, entitled 'Dawn of Democracy', Aegisthus, dressed in morning clothes, swings away at a punch ball and declaims, in couplets, on the difficulty of being president in an ungrateful time:

> Ladies and Gentlemen, it's easy to sneer,
> But try to do better than I do here . . .
> In any case, have any of you governed before?
>   (punches ball violently)
> Immediately, Right and Left try to settle their score.
> The morning papers' attacks draw blood,
> Caricaturists fling mud,
> One is shadowed, spied upon, mocked!
> The whole thing's lost its romance,

132

The hero's pose, the grand gestures and stance.
One can't 'crown it' anymore or 'throne it' anymore,
In a word, it's hardly worth it anymore!
Be it Werfel or Romain Rolland,
It is established that spiritual ways
Don't even attract a cat these days.
If you side with the intellectuals,
There's an immediate putsch by the Dada rebels.
One doesn't want to be dragged through the mire . . .
One gulps down corn flour and cocaine,
Does a couple of hours of exercise a day,
Calls it 'My System' for building-up muscular strength.
Finally one notices with a sad frown,
That the 'goodness' of people has again let you down.

At this point, the Dadaists, who were sitting unnoticed in the front row, went into action. Grosz and Hülsenbeck had specially donned iron crosses for the event. In true Dada fashion, they started protesting loudly about the programme, which, in effect, had been marred by terrible acoustics, yelled 'Long live art! Down with Reinhardt!' Some of the audience were apparently unaware that the creators of the programme were largely Dadaists and that this protest was part of the 'entertainment', for shouts of 'Out with the Dadaists' could be heard. However, when no bodily effort was made to eject the Dadaists, Hülsenbeck himself got up and shouted: 'What kind of order is this here. Where then is the police who are to kick us out?' This part of the evening dissolved in laughter and rumpus.

Apart from the *Simply Classical!* parody, the Schall und Rauch programme contained a variety of elements. There were film screenings, the first of which was a cartoon film designed by Walter Trier, of a day in the life of the Reich president. Holländer played a piano accompaniment to this, and Klabund recited poetry. There were dance presentations, satirical monologue parodies by Gustav von Wagenheim – whose technique Brecht studied – and of course, song: the Schall und Rauch team introduced some of the period's most famous song performers.

One of these was Paul Grätz. An 'Urberliner' – original Berliner – with protruding nose and workman's cap, he could sing Berlin dialect as no one else. It was through him that Mehring's quickly-paced, slangy city chansons became popular. Grätz, a master of improvisation, would add rhyming couplets or quips to whatever he was singing or performing, and thereby make a topical point or bring his audience directly into the act. He was a brilliant monologuist, inspiring the texts written for him as much as interpreting them. Mehring testifies that Grätz could 'create whole novels in ten minutes'. A deep belief in democracy was evident in all that he performed, and the stage increasingly became for him a combat ground against Nazism. He was forced to leave Germany with the Nazi accession to power, and died soon afterwards, some say of sorrow for the state of his native land.

The singer and monologuist Paul Grätz. Kurt Tucholsky Archiv.

133

SCHALL UND RAUCH

EINFACH KLASSISCH

Grosz-Heartfield mont.

ADOLPH FÜRSTNER BERLIN W.

Gussy Holl was another of the Schall und Rauch team. Elegantly vampish, with a plastic voice and acting ability which had been tested on Reinhardt's large stage, she had a genius for parody and inspired some of Tucholsky's most popular songs. He wrote of her, 'Frankfurt has produced two great men: Goethe and Gussy Holl . . . She can do anything: hate and love, stroke and beat, sing and speak – there is no tone that is not part of her lyre.' Dressed as a 'slightly pregnant' American Salvation Army girl, Gussy Holl used to sing a bilingual parody of the contemporary love lyric written by Mehring. The song incorporates the whole American and jazz cults in what became the standard semi-satirical, semi-romantic tone.

Opposite
Schall und Rauch programme designed by George Grosz and John Heartfield for *Einfach Klassisch!* (Simply Classical!) 1919. Courtesy Heartfield Archiv.

> *If the man in the moon*
> *were a coon and im Dunkeln liebten die Girls*
> *Schenkten alle weissen Ladys*
> *Schwarze Babys*
> *Schwarzen Kerls.*
> *Please kuss mich rein –*
> *Lass mich ein,*
> *Black boy, o my black boy*
> *In the Niggerparadies, in the Niggerparadies.*

> If the man in the moon
> were a coon and the girls loved in the dark,
> All the white ladies
> Would make gifts of
> black babies
> to black guys,
> Kiss me clean –
> Let me in,
> Black boy, oh my black boy
> In the niggerparadise . . .

Tucholsky wrote 'Petronella' for Gussy Holl, a marvellously naughty parody of the prevailing Berlin trend for nudity on the stage, and simultaneously a laughing dig at the amusement cabarets,

> *Nicht bei Lulu nur oder Wedekind*
> *Ist der Platz für Deine Reize,*
> *denn je nackter Deine Schultern sind,*
> *je mehr sage man: 'Det kleid se!' . . .*

> *Als Iphigenie trägst Du nur*
> *'ne Armbanduhr, 'ne Armbanduhr,*
> *ich seh den weissen Nacken,*
> *wie schön sind Deine Backen! . . .*

> *Zieh dich aus, Petronella, zieh dich aus!*
> *Denn du darfst nicht ennuyant sein*
> *und nur so wirst du bekannt sein;*
> *und es jubelt voller Lust das ganze Haus:*
> *'Zieh dich aus, Petronella, zieh dich aus!'*

Not only Lulu or Wedekind
Provide a setting for your charms,
For the more you bare your arms,
The more people purr, 'Cor! It suits 'er!

As Iphigenia you didn't wear much
But a wrist watch, a wrist watch.
I see your neck glistening white,
How lovely those cheeks might be to bite!

Strip Petronella strip!
Oh, don't be so tedious
Fame comes with teasing us,
And lustfully the whole house let rip:
'Strip Petronella strip!'

While Gussy Holl was the Schall und Rauch's sophisticated coquette, Blandine Ebinger was its slender, braided *arme Mädchen*, the poor little street girl who had all the knowledge and all the innocence of the big city. Friedrich Holländer spotted her as his muse, even before the cabaret's opening night, and within a few months they were married, forming an unforgettable team. Blandine Ebinger's physical expressiveness, her ability to become totally the matter of her song and suggest the comic and the tragic at once, made her the perfect vehicle for Holländer's street-dialect songs.

*Wo Mutter wäscht, im Vorderhaus,
da is et mir jeschehn.
Da lag een Jroschen uffm Tisch
und hat mir anjesehn.
Frau Wischnak jing mal 'raus, wat holn –
der Jroschen, der lag da.
Und plötzlich hatt' ick ihn jestohln –
Weiss nich, wie det jeschah.
Wie bin ick bloss dazu jekomm'.
det ick det Jeld hab' wechjenomm'?
Een Jroschen liegt auf meiner Ehre,
een Jroschen, unscheinbar und kleen.
Wenn ick't bloss nich jewesen wäre.
Ich kann mir jar nich mehr in Spiegel sehn.*

Where Mum does the washin',
That's where it happened to me.
There was a sixpence on the table,
And it seemed to beckon me.
Frau Wischnak went out to fetch somethin'
And the sixpence still lay there.
And suddenly I pinched it –
Don't know how it happened, I swear.
How under the sun
Could I take the money and run?
Now between my honour and me,

Ringelnatz, Kuttel-Daddeldu and his children, by Karl Arnold.

Lies a sixpence slight and small.
If only I hadn't been the one to do it.
Can't face myself in the mirror at all.

In 1920 the Schall und Rauch's most outstanding visiting performer
was Joachim Ringelnatz. Back from the war and more global travels,
Ringelnatz had begun writing his adventure-packed poems about the
sailor Kuttel-Daddeldu. This tough boozing character, with his
slangy mixture of languages, was a perfect post-war hero. A kin of
Grosz, Brecht and Ben Traven's murderers and gangsters, he emerged
from the lawless romantic underworld – which reflected the generally
anarchic tone of the times – to appear on the cabaret stage:

As Daddeldu travelled through the world wide,
It often happened that here and there
One or t'other of his children he spied,
who warmly welcomed their Europapa:
'Gud morning! Sdrastwuide! – Bong Jur, Daddeldü!
Bont tscherno! Ok phosphor! Tsching-tschung! Bablabü!'
And Daddeldu thanked them touched and glad,
Dipped deep into his trouser pocket,
Happily gave them whatever he had,
   – Whiskey, by the bucket,
Matches, opium, tobacco turkish,
bullets and bandages for maladies murkish,
Gave each one two dollars and smiled, 'Ei, ei!'
And disappeared, waving good-bye.

Needless to say the patriotic press was outraged. But the majority of the audience waited in tense expectation for Kuttel-Daddeldu's next adventure.

The Schall und Rauch only sustained its artistic programme for a year, before being hit by inflation and degenerating into an amusement club. During that time it presented a programme which finds its closest English equivalent in the BBC's *That was the Week that Was* of 1962: witty investigative journalism, experimental sketches, and functional poetry, spoken or sung, all with a hefty dose of satire.

Rosa Valetti. Kurt Tucholsky Archiv.

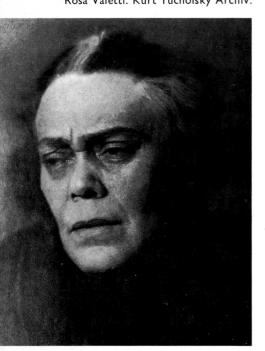

Rosa Valetti and the cabaret Grössenwahn

Among the many performers which the Schall und Rauch thrust into the limelight, one, Rosa Valetti, went on to pioneer her own cabaret.

Certainly the most powerful of the cabaret's female performers, Rosa Valetti was dedicated to the idea that the small stage had to be used for political and social criticism. An actress and authentic *diseuse*, with mobile features, flaming eyes, and red hair, she would belt out her songs in a trumpet-like voice which could convey the horrors of the past war as well as the plight of the present.

Rosa Valetti opened her cabaret in the Café Grössenwahn (Megalomania), literary headquarters for the Expressionists, and indeed, as the name suggests, for all aspiring poets. The programme was determined by her temperament and consisted of a rich mixture of political chansons, from Bruant to Tucholsky, and sketches. Many of the Schall und Rauch performers appeared here, and Valetti added her own discovery, Kate Kühl, to their list. With a deep mannish voice, robust personality, and gift for improvisation, Kate Kühl was the perfect vehicle for the ballads about seamen which were so plentiful in the time. Brecht's 'Surrabaya Johnny', which Kühl performed, is part of this tradition. Erich Kästner wrote a parody of it, which she fearlessly performed, sending up both herself and Brecht's vaunted debt to Kipling.

138

You came out of the Pirna wood.
You didn't say 'Miss', but 'tart'.
Like a sailor you were all tattooed.
There was nothing warm in your heart.
You said you had taken many a trip,
And were travelling overland to your ship,
That you had muscles made of steel,
And besides that, you had a great deal.

That took gall, Johnny.
I fell for it all, Johnny!
You lied Johnny. You're just not straight.
You never travelled, Johnny.
You're not from Kipling, Johnny!
Take that pipe out of your mouth, man:
You're from Brecht!

The Grössenwahn was hit by the inflation, like its predecessor, and for a while Rosa Valetti undertook the direction of the Rakete only to move from there to a second personal venture, the Rampe. Here, to an already highly political programme, she added the work and performance of Erich Weinert, whose poems and songs were directly dedicated to revolution. Towards the end of the twenties, Valetti was one of the initiators of the Larifari, a radically satirical cabaret which moved from locale to locale, and numbered among its text writers, Frederick Gotfurt, later to be a leading figure in the London exile cabaret and the film world.

Trude Hesterberg. Kurt Tucholsky Archiv.

Trude Hesterberg's Wild Stage

From 1921 to 1924, Trude Hesterberg, a *diseuse* of diverse talents, ran the Wild Stage, one of Berlin's most pungent literary cabarets. Her team included Mehring, Tucholsky, Klabund and Max Herrmann-Neisse, all of whom wrote and performed songs, poems and satires for the cabaret, with the exception of Tucholsky. Her performers also included Werner Richard Heymann, who served as house composer and pianist; and a score of performers and singers, some already well known, some discovered by the tireless Hesterberg.

One of the best-loved parts of her programme was a circus-like satirical sketch performed by Wilhelm Bendow called 'The Tattooed Lady'. Covered in tattoo-decorated plaster of Paris, Bendow would appear on stage looking something like a mammoth female wrestler competing for the title of Miss World. Then, in a quick-running monologue, he would boast to the audience of how the entirety of his body was covered with tattoos, except for one tiny part on which the medical men had forbidden such mosaic work. The audience was invited on a verbal tour of this remarkable anatomy, on which all the greats of the world were desirous of being recorded. 'On the topmost level of the back of my thigh, I bear Germany's war heroes; at the

139

edge, the famous expedition leader, Ludendorff. On the topmost level of the back of my right thigh, the Decline of the West. In the background, the Black Forest. ...' A trip around the Tattooed Lady's body was a thorough journey through contemporary Germany.

To performers such as Rosa Valetti, Blandine Ebinger, Paul Grätz, Gussy Holl, Kate Kühl, and Kurt Gerron, Hesterberg added Margo Lion, a model-thin singer whose talents for satirizing high fashion were a great hit with the audience, and Annemarie Hase, a madcap, singing comedienne. She delivered Mehring's 'The Fortune-Teller', a sinister spoof of the illicit abortion industry and of Berlin's barbarous underworld.

She gazed into the coffee-ground
Where the rich husbands would be found,
She lived in a dingy basement-cellar,
The Fortune-teller.

Her help could readily be bought
For a poor girl, what had been 'caught'.
Don't worry, she'd say, I'll do it, Honey,
Give me the money.

She kept a goldfish and a cat
And a strong-box beneath her bed
In her dingy, smelly basement-cellar,
The Fortune-teller.

Elli, the slut, came late one night
'Bloody Tommy done it,' she cried.
'I won't carry his bastard. It's no good
I dread motherhood.'

The greedy witch told her at once
To come without her cruel ponce
She would help Elli, down in the cellar,
The Fortune-teller.

That night there was a dreadful sound,
The pussy-cat went round and round,
Then it chose the empty money-casket
As sleeping-basket.

Three days passed. They broke in and found
Tied like a parcel, gagged and bound
In her smelly, dingy basement-cellar,
The Fortune-teller.

Before the judge the cruel pair
Denied the deed – it wasn't fair.
When the victim's wound re-started bleeding
There was no pleading.

Justice was done. Remains to tell
They all met merrily in hell
Which she found much hotter than her cellar
The Fortune-teller.
(translated by Dorothea Gotfurt)

140

Trude Hesterberg, too, was one of Mehring's great interpreters. In his autobiography, Holländer evokes her as the new Yvette Guilbert, a woman who could intone the harshly satirical tones of Mehring's 'Stock-Exchange Song' or 'The Prostitute Press', as well as whimsical chansons. On top of this, Hesterberg had a genuine nose for talent. Ringelnatz appeared on her stage and it was she who first introduced the young Brecht, then a Munich resident, to the Berlin public. On the evening of the very day he had come to audition before her, Hesterberg had Brecht perform on the Wild Stage. That night it truly lived up to its name. Brecht appeared before the audience in an ill-fitting suit and carrying a banjo. He sang his 'Legend of the Dead Soldier' in a shrill, aggressive monotone and by the end of the third stanza, the audience, several Junkers among them, was in uproar. Sekt-glasses were hurled on stage along with insults, and Hesterberg was forced to let the curtain fall on the young writer. Acting as conférencier, Mehring (who tells the tale) confronted the audience. He marched on stage and told the public that a discreditable event had taken place that evening, not for the performer Brecht, but for them, the public. They would one day remember that they had been present on this occasion.

Cabaret for revolution

While the literary cabarets presented a satirical critique of contemporary events, they always mingled this criticism with humour and a certain artistry. The aggressive overtones of Brecht's performance in the Wild Stage, were only echoed in one Berlin cabaret of note, the Küka or Künstler-Café. This cabaret functioned as a meeting place for a young literary bohemia which was becoming increasingly revolutionary in its politics as the decade neared its end. The programme at the Küka was generally improvised and acts or readings arose in response to discussion and audience demand. Largely made up of left-wing literary intellectuals, this public was 'in the know' and the performers could assume a certain like-thinking on its part. Performances at the Küka sometimes took on the aspect of agit-prop rehearsals intended for further presentation elsewhere.

Among the Küka's notables was the conférencier, writer, actor and pioneering broadcaster, Karl Schnog, who appeared in all of Berlin's best cabarets. He not only read his verse, but held a running, sharply satirical, commentary on the contemporary situation, always emphasizing the battle against reactionary forces. In Dachau, Sachsenhausen and Buchenwald, the camps where he spent most of the Hitler years, Schnog organized cabaret evenings, occurrences which in retrospect, take on almost mythical proportions.

Ernst Toller, a principal actor in Munich's revolutionary republic, was another of the Küka's participants. But basically this cabaret took its imprint from Erich Weinert, a revolutionary poet whose work was a vehicle for class agitation. A trade-school teacher, Weinert had come to Berlin specifically because he had heard of the Küka and wanted to recite his poems directly to people. With his arrival the cabaret drew to itself an increasingly radical clientele and in 1930 Weinert was forbidden to perform and the cabaret to continue its presentations. Weinert's verse, directed against Social Democrats, and academic leftists and towards outright confrontation, was overtly agitational. Here is a fragment of one of his poems, a straightforward attack on the Weimar Republic and its ruling powers, 'The Carnival Parade of the Republic':

> Tshingtshing! Bumbum! Tatutata!
> Heading the march is Grandpapa[1]
> A pocket hanky black-white-red,
> Mock neutrality till he's dead!
>   And then the German economy.
>
> Herr Hilferding,[2] stern in the fore,
> Sports his old frock-coat of yore.
> With him gentlemen of capital,
> Celebrating their Lo-carnival.[3]
>   And then the military spirit
>
> Herr Groener[4] advances, sword in hand,
> Gift from Gessler,[5] former head of the band.
> On every breast, metal galore,
> A cheer bursts forth, a thunderous roar.
>   And then the church fathers.
>
> Now come Germany's hanging judges,
> A Christian coat over their grudges,
> Too large in front, too short in back,
> Just doesn't fit and that's that . . .
> Quick some music to unite them all,
> A Republican dance for carnival.
> But this too must come to a close,
> And then the slop laps round our toes.
>   And then comes something else.
>
> Eyes left, they're on their way,
> Millions of boys in field grey.
> Your stupid plodding masked trance,
> Will soon be turned into death's dance.
>   The masquerade is over.

Most of the writers so far mentioned were left-wing in their politics but unaffiliated to any party. Weinert was an exception and dedicated his poetry to the service of the Communist Party. He participated

[1] Von Hindenburg, Reich President 1925–1934.
[2] Minister of finance, 1928–29.
[3] A pun on treaty of Locarno.
[4] General Groener, Defence Minister 1928–32.
[5] Otto Gessler, former Defence Minister.

in the *Red Revue*, directed by Piscator, who went on to produce some of the most inflammatory and technically innovative spectacles of the twenties. The *Red Revue* was aimed at a working-class public, and Weinert's success in this production resulted in his giving more and more of his energies to recitations at workers meetings and political assemblies. As he himself reminisces, his poetry increasingly became a propaganda medium intended to agitate the audience into action. The bitterness of Weinert's satire and the rage which exuded from his work pushed the cabaret over the brink of entertainment into desperation and fanaticism.

The Blue Bird

At the other extreme from the Küka, was the Blue Bird, a cabaret which placed artistry far above political commitment. It was run by one of the many groups of Russian émigrés who sought refuge in the Berlin of the twenties. Under the leadership of Jushnij, this cabaret produced not only its own multi-national language – a mixture of Russian, French, English and German clothed in the rhythms and intonation of the last – but a presentation style which mingled Russian folklore with the stage equivalents of Constructivism and Cubism. The group used real actors, partially hidden by cardboard cut-outs, ingenious stage decor, pantomime and music, and invented sketches

A folkloric sketch from the *Blue Bird* Cabaret. Klaus Budzinski Archiv.

which could either capture the mechanized dehumanization of contemporary life, or evoke the magic of a child's book of fairy-tales. The actors were highly stylized in their gestures, emerging either as marionette-like dolls, or robots.

One famous sketch, entitled 'Volga Boatmen' had seven actors miming the weary progress of rowing a boat upstream. Their exaggerated gestural misery was accompanied by a mourning song and the lament of a violin. The whole scene was set against a painted sunset. What emerged was not a realistic representation but a piece of pure fantasy or acted fairy-tale. In another tableau, 'Sofaklatsch', Cubist-like female torsos piled on a huge sofa, perform a song. Only mouths and faces move in this two-dimensionality where beings have become objects. 'Time is Money', a representation of the machine-like life of Americans, logically brings this cliché to the point of absurdity. The American, a man-robot, woos a female robot to the rapid ticking of a clock. She rejects him. He immediately shoots himself, only to find in the mechanized course of things that his inner clock is working again. The action is repeated, and this time round his courtship is successful.

Acting as a genially ironical conférencier Jushnij bridged the distance between the stylized world on stage and reality. In his comical German, he would bait the audience and bring them out of passive reverie into active participation. 'Instead of "*da capo*" please say in Russian, "*Jeschtscho ras*",' he would urge his public, and when a member of the audience succeeded in doing this, he would mutter, 'Oh, you speak such good Russian. You must be from Charlottenburg,' or Liverpool, or Rouen, as the case might be when the company toured Europe. Another of his quips: 'I have experienced a great many German audiences, in Dresden, in Hamburg, in Berlin, but I must admit tonight's public is the best we have ever had. Of course, I say this every night.' Provocational tactics, mild or bitter, always remained a part of authentic cabaret performance, whatever the style or content of the particular presentation.

Relatives and Progeny of Cabaret

In the mid-twenties Germany's cabarets spawned an offspring: the cabaretistic satirical revue. Abandoning intimate space so as to gain a slightly larger audience, these revues incorporated the satirical tone of the cabaret, often softened its sharpness and political critique just a little, dropped the improvisational flavour, and introduced a loose, thematic continuity into the sequence of acts and sketches. Verbal wit generally, but not always, played a secondary role to music and dance.

The musical revue had, of course, a pre-war history in Germany and one of its major creators, the composer Rudolf Nelson, had enlisted the collaboration of Tucholsky, as well as of many of the best cabaret performers. His revues had that mixture of the capricious, the racy, erotic and sentimental which Tucholsky was always drawn to. But while Nelson saw the appearance of Josephine Baker as the climax of his revues, when Mischa Spoliansky and Friedrich Holländer, the cabaret's most important musical men, turned to the revue form, they emphasized that satirical spirit and political wit which was the essence of post-war cabaret. Thus the cabaret satirical revue, with its jazzy, parodistic, catchy, music was born. From the mid-twenties on, Berlin was entertained – some say enlightened – by such spectacles.

Holländer alone produced eighteen revues, beginning with *Laterna Magica – also a revue*. Mischa Spoliansky and Marcellus Schiffer collaborated on the extremely popular, *Es liegt in der Luft*, It's in the air; and the cabaretistic revue began to be adapted by various directors for their own purposes.

Piscator's use of the revue form is in many ways the most interesting. Intent on making it into a political and proletarian form which would both analyse the contemporary situation and advocate a socialist future, Piscator urged that all possible theatrical elements be exploited: music, song, acrobatics, sport, film, statistics, harangue, even on-stage drawing – initially done by Grosz. For the 1924 elections, Piscator prepared the *Red Revel Revue*, which brought a variety of these elements into play as part of the continuing topical debate between proletarian and bourgeois. The revue begins with strife in the audience: two workers are arguing loudly over their situation. A bourgeois in top-hat interferes, and asks the two men to spend an evening with him. Only then does the curtain rise on the first scene. Piscator's scenes moved quickly and were connected by the continuing debate which bourgeois and workers carried on between them. These scenes were also interspersed with bits of film, or statistics flashed on a screen.

George Grosz set-design for Piscator's production of *The Good Soldier Schweik*, 1928.

In his second 'red revue', *Trotz Alledem!* or Despite all that!, Piscator presented a history of the years between 1914 and 1919. Using all the elements of the first production, this revue acted as a documentary montage of the war years and was intended as agitprop. But Piscator's work, his influence on Brecht and on stage production generally, demands an entire book to be evaluated properly.

Claire Waldoff

Whatever the intent of the German revue producers, this form drew on the talents of all the major cabaret performers and writers. One of these performers, Claire Waldoff, had a following which stretched from the most popular to the most sophisticated. Her career began with a censor's edict: the scene in which she was to appear in the pre-war revue *Rudolf of Berlin*, was cut out of the show because of its supposed anti-militaristic content. Furthermore, the Eton-boy suit which she wore for her performance was deemed unsuitable by the police, since it was forbidden then for women to appear 'dressed as men' after eleven in the evening.

Undaunted by this set-back, this slight gamine from Hanover educated herself in Berlinese and became one of Germany's leading folk-singers and satirical *diseuses*. Here is her pre-war dialect 'hit' song, 'Hermann is his Name':

> *Hermann heesst er!*
> *Wie der Mann knutschen, drücken, küssen kann.*
> *Druffgänger kenn' ich schon viele,*
> *aber so schnell kam zum Ziele*
> *keenr noch. Ja, der is Meester.*
> *Hermann heesst er! . . .*
>
> *Hermann heesst er!*
> *Ooch zum Ball*
> *führte er mir neulich mal.*
> *Der kann wackeln, knicken, schieben,*
> *'rull und 'rum, mal hier, mal drüben;*
> *mit die Knie manchmal stösst er:*
> *Hermann heesst er!*

Herman's 'is name!
'Ow this man can smooch, press and kiss.
I know many men of action,
But none make it as quickly as this,
Yeh, 'e's the master.
Herman 'e is!

Herman's 'is name!
Even took me to a ball
last fall.
Oh how he can bend, sway, twirl
Up and down with a girl;
Sometimes 'e makes a pass with 'is knees
Herman, please.

With the Nazi accession to power, the Hermann of Claire's song became associated with Hermann Goering, and the piece took on political connotations as a dissenting spoof. Its performance was banned, but the brave Waldoff continued to perform this 'anonymous' addition to it, claiming that it had nothing to do with her 'hit', since it originated with the people.

Claire Waldoff. Kurt Tucholsky Archiv.

Rechts Lametta, links Lametta,
Un der Bauch wird imma fetta,
Un in Preussen is er Meester.
Hermann heesst er!

Medals left, medals right-er
And his paunch grows ever wide-er
And in Prussia he's Gauleiter
Herman, Heil to'm.

Valeska Gert

A somewhat different kind of artist was Valeska Gert, a woman who could justly be called the inventor of the social-critical dance pantomime. Her first dance appearance on the Berlin stage caused a sensation. Dressed in flaming colours, this woman with dramatic, almost ugly, features performed a frenzied expressionistic dance. There were shouts of pornography and at the next performance the police were present. But Valeska Gert had been warned, and for that one evening she toned her movements down somewhat.

An actress as well as a dancer, she began to create dance presentations in which every part of her body was used to enact a state of being or a character. This is her own description of her death-agony dance:

Motionless, I stand in long black shirt on a glaringly lit podium. My body tenses itself slowly, the struggle begins; my hands tighten into fists, my shoulders hunch up, my face is distorted by pain. The

147

Valeska Gert on stage. Courtesy Dr Robert Steinfeld.

pain becomes unbearable, my mouth opens wide to utter a silent cry. I bend my head back; shoulders, arms, hands, my whole body grows numb. I try to defend myself. Senseless. For a few seconds, I stand there motionless, a column of pain. Then slowly, the life drains out of my body. Very slowly it relaxes. The pain leaves, the mouth becomes softer. My shoulders fall; arms and hands grow limp . . . My head falls quickly, the head of a doll. Finished. Gone. I am dead.

Not surprisingly, Valeska Gert speaks of always being in a state of trance, eyes tightly shut, when dancing.

Such presentations alternated in her repertory with satirical dance mimes. In 'Canaille' she created the figure of a sensitive whore for the first time on the dance stage, her every motion signifying the way in which her body had been exploited for money. Brecht asked her to perform this dance in his Red Grape cabaret. When she asked him to explain what he meant by 'epic theatre', his answer apparently, was, 'What you do.' Indeed, Valeska Gert's radical innovations, her grotesque highly stylized body gestures, could be thought of as 'alienation' techniques. She was applauded in Russia and throughout Europe, and also performed in the Schall und Rauch; and along with Helene Weigel and Lotte Lenya, in one of the red revues Brecht participated in. The Russians had termed her dance a form of agitprop. In the early thirties, she opened her own cabaret, the *Kohlkopp*. Despite the excellence of some of its performances and her own unfailing ingenuity, this ran aground because of her inability to keep accounts. Her second attempt at launching a cabaret took place in New York, during her wartime exile there. The Beggars' Bar is still remembered in America as a unique project.

The People's comics: Enter Karl Valentin

In their search for the popular, the cabaretists turned not only to song and functional poetry, but to the people's theatre. Berlin had its own slapstick genius in the comedian Erich Carow, an actor-director who ran a popular theatre with his family in the city's equivalent of the East End. Heinrich Mann discovered Carow and lauded his ability to portray the 'little man' to perfection. The troupe was invited to 'tour' the 'West End' and became the rage of the intellectual and cabaret set, only to find after a brief time that the sophisticates preferred to see it in the 'East End'.

Carow's natural comic talents were only equalled by the now near-legendary Karl Valentin. Munich's answer to Charlie Chaplin, Valentin performed in beer halls; small and large, popular and highbrow theatres; as well as on the cabaret stage. His art, that of a unique folk comedian, falls somewhere between music hall and literary theatre. Thus, he was adopted by that middle form, the cabaret.

Gangly limbed and rubber-faced, as tall, thin, and slope-shouldered as a question mark, Valentin had the sad eyes and look of a classic tragic clown. Valentin used features and physique to the best possible comic advantage whether masquerading in tatty blond wig, under-shirt and gauzy skirt as a lyre-strumming Lorelei; or dressed in the contemporary outfit of a cyclist. The underlying tone of all his work – monologues, farcical songs, sketches or one act plays done in conjunction with his disciple and partner, Liesl Karlstadt – is that of the be-devilled little man, constantly harrassed by the flexible illogicality of language, by bureacratic hierarchies, by technology, indeed by the most ordinary aspects of everyday life. Valentin's genius lay in his drawing the most extraordinary consequences from ordinary events, or ideas. Logic toppled over into the absurd and with its disappearance, a new perspective emerged on language, institutions, events, or class prejudices. Here is an excerpt from a sketch called *Tingeltangel* in which Valentin plays a kettledrummer in a suburban band. His masterly usage of the Munich idiom, which grows ever more slurred as the sketch progresses, is unfortunately lost in the translation. This, then, is to be read with either a brilliant cockney comic or Groucho Marx in mind:

Valentin: Has Anderl told you about it yet?

Conductor: Wha. . . What does he want now?

Valentin: Just think of it, yesterday we experienced a real coincidence. I and Anderl, we went yesterday to Kaufinger Street and happened to be speaking of a cyclist. And at that very same instant, as we were speaking of a cyclist, one just chanced to come along.

Conductor: Yes – and?

Valentin: What – and?

Conductor: Where's the coincidence?

Valentin: I said we were speaking of a cyclist, and at that same instant, as we were speaking of a cyclist, one came along!

Conductor: Yes – and what then happened with this cyclist? What did he do then?

Valentin: Nothing! He rode on.

Conductor: Well, where's the coincidence then?

Valentin: That's the coincidence!

Conductor: But there's no coincidence in that cyclist there! That's absolutely nothing. Nothing!

Valentin: Not even a cyclist?

Conductor: No, I mean, that's no coincidence when a cyclist appears on Kaufinger Street. There are about a thousand cyclists a day there.

Valentin: No, only one came along.

Conductor: I mean that at just about every metre another cyclist comes along.

Valentin: Yes, but not when one is speaking about it.

Conductor: Ach! You should have been speaking of something quite different.

Valentin: But we weren't speaking of anything else.

Conductor: I know that already – I only mean, that if for example you had been speaking of a pilot.

Valentin: But we weren't. We were speaking of a cyclist.

Conductor: I know that – I mean if you had been speaking of a pilot and at the same time, one suddenly came along above you, that really would have been a coincidence!

Valentin: Ya – but we didn't look up.

Conductor: I only mean – if instead of speaking of a cyclist, you had been speaking of a pilot . . .

Valentin: What do you mean? How can I be speaking of a pilot when I'm talking about a cyclist.

Conductor: I mean – in the same way that you were speaking of a cyclist, you could have been speaking of a pilot.

Valentin: Impossible!

Conductor: Wha. . haven't you ever spoken of a pilot in your life yet?

Valentin: Often, but not then . . . then we were only speaking of a cyclist.

Conductor: Now leave me in peace. I don't want to hear anymore from you.

Valentin: Alright. Tomorrow we're going for a walk again. We'll talk about a pilot . . . But woe to you, if a cyclist comes along!

Valentin's twisted logic, as Hans Mayer called his style, indeed his entire relationship to his beer-drinking audience, had a formative influence on Brecht. The two worked together on several occasions, and Brecht's early one-act plays, such as *The Wedding*, clearly bear Valentin's stamp. As Brecht's critics have pointed out, what drew him to Valentin was the comic's use of an estranged or alienated thinking process, which propelled the audience into seeing the ordinary in a new light.

Karl Valentin. Institüt Für Theaterwissen-Schaft, University of Cologne.

151

Wie sieht Hitler aus?

(Th. Th. Heine)

Adolf Hitler läßt sich nie abbilden. Bei meinem Aufenthalt in Berlin wurde ich mit Fragen über sein Aussehen bestürmt.

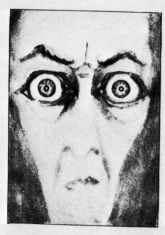
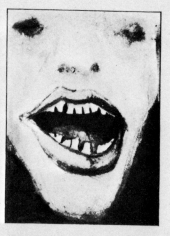

„Ist es wahr, daß er in der Öffentlichkeit nur mit einer schwarzen Gesichtsmaske erscheint?"

„Das Charakteristische seines Gesichts sind doch wohl die faszinierenden Augen?"

„Oder ist der Mund die Hauptsache?"

„Oder die Nase?"

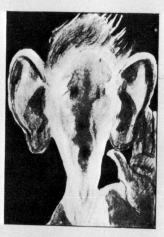

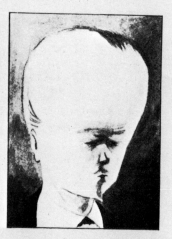

„Trägt er vielleicht einen wallenden Bart wie Wotan oder wie Rabindranath Tagore?"

„Er hört die leisesten Äußerungen der Volksstimme; sind nicht seine Ohren besonders entwickelt?"

„Verrät etwa die untere Gesichtshälfte seine fabelhafte Energie?"

„Oder finden die ungeheuren geistigen Fähigkeiten ihren Ausdruck in fast hypertrophischen Schädelformen?"

„Ist er fett?"

„Ist er mager?"

„Ist er schön?"

Die Fragen mußten unbeantwortet bleiben. Hitler ist überhaupt kein Individuum. Er ist ein Zustand. Nur der Futurist kann ihn bildlich darstellen.

Into the Third Reich

Valentin's detestation of Hitler's politics was never overtly evident in his sketches. Nevertheless, the overall tone of his acts was enough to label him an 'enemy of Nazism', and he was not permitted to perform during the Hitler era. This fate, however, was a mild one in comparison to those cabaret conférenciers who levelled a daily attack on Nazism and who became victims of Nazi terror.

The role of the conférencier was a complex and manifold one. Not only was he, like a master of ceremonies, to introduce acts and set the tone for performances which, in themselves, might be extremely modest; but he also had to be able to draw the audience into the spectacle and provide a quick repartee to any challenge it might make. Besides this, the best conférenciers had to be well versed in literature, masters of improvisation, and antennae for the next day's news. Witty forecasters of tomorrows events, critical journalists who could provide a running satirical commentary on the state of the world, these conférenciers were the essence of the Kabarett. Of the many who developed an individual style and rose to prominence in the heyday of the cabaret, a few achieved such mastery of the conférence form, that it became in itself a satirical act which could be incorporated into cabaret programmes.

Although satire was proved to be a weapon too weak to launch a victorious assault on Nazism, the wit of the conférenciers emerged as a survival tactic in the early days of Hitler's power. The particular turn of cabaret wit is evident in the following examples of conférencier humour:

An *SA man* baiting a Jew: 'Tell me Jew, who's responsible for the fact that we lost the war?'
The Jew: 'The Jewish generals, of course.'
SA man: 'Good, good.' (Then reflecting a little) . . . 'But we didn't have any Jewish generals.'
The Jew: 'Not us – the others!'

A conférencier, raising his arm to the level of a 'Heil', looks up at it questioningly: 'That's how high we are in shit . . .'

Opposite
'What does Hitler Look Like?' 1923 strip by Th. Th. Heine in *Simplicissimus*. The strip suggests that it is impossible to represent Hitler graphically or answer questions about his most striking features. Only the Futurist could depict Hitler, states the final caption, for he is not an individual but a condition.

Kabarett der Komiker

Berlin's largest and longest-lasting cabaret was the Kabarett der Komiker. It provided a platform for many conférenciers and indeed rose to artistic prominence because of them. This cabaret, which had its own long-running comic weekly called *Die Frechheit*, Impudence, was a show place for the 'stars'. Yvette Guilbert sang here. From America came Nina Mae McKinney, the wife of King Vidor, and Alex Hyde with his 'Twelve Jazz Girls'. And there were Germany's own celebrities: Ilse Bois, the cabaret's favourite, among whose other talents was a genius for detailed parody; Rosa Valetti; Paul Grätz doing his monologues of street hawkers and postmen; and Roda Roda, the Viennese master of the anecdote. The famed singer Ernst Busch, whose more usual stage was that of the revolutionary cabarets, red revues or workers' rallies, performed here as well. One of his most moving numbers was Robert Gilbert's '*Stempellied*' or the Dole Song, which captures the horrors of the Depression:

Ilse Bois in a sketch at the *Kabarett der Komiker*. Courtesy Theater-Museum, Munich.

Not a copper in your pocket
Just the dole-card, man.
Through the holes in your torn jacket
Peeps the sun – and then
You look at the world and frown.
You don't have a bean.
You drop dead – you just fall down,
Nobody sheds a tear.
And no guv'nor seein' you in this mess
Would stand you a Guinness –
Only in the morgue, you kinda
have a meagre chance.
Even if you join the queue
For the dole, my son,
It's no bloody good to you
You have had it, chum.

Without work, without a pad
You don't count for nought.
Like a fly stuck to the window
You will be squashed out.
Without work and without lolly
You don't count at all,
And the fat man swears, 'By Golly,
Don't come near me . . .'
Society will throw you quickly
To the dogs old chap.
If you're hungry, if you're sickly
Better shut your trap.

Soon the bones will be protruding
From your skin, and then
Within weeks you'll know for certain:
You have had it man.
For your last few marks you buy
yourself some planks of wood.
You only need a narrow coffin
And that, at least, is good.
Don't you hurry,
Don't you worry,
You'll meet the angels soon enough,

And the unions
And the nation,
Will bless rationalization
When they see you out.
To be on the safe side then,
Join the dole queue pretty soon
For you'll remain a poor man,
High up there beyond the moon!
    (translated by Dorothea Gotfurt)

Nina Mae Mckinney on stage. Courtesy Theater-Museum, Munich.

Gutenberg is aghast at the use his press has been put to. 'This is not what I intended,' he exclaims in this 1922 inflation cartoon. *Simplicissimus*.

Opposite
The hated 'Spiesser' or Babbit character as seen by *Jugend*'s Josef Gauer, 1930. For the *Spiesser*, it was said, the only suitable form of government is dictatorship.

But the overall tone of the Kade Ko, as it was known, would have been that of a structured and formalized American nightclub – a performance locale which mixes a great deal of kitsch with a few genuinely literary or satirical acts – had it not been for the conférenciers. These men raised the programme beyond entertainment and launched a nightly satirical attack against the forces of reaction.

Vienna's Fritz Grünbaum, the small stage's wittiest conversationalist, was known at the time as the 'philosophical' conférencier. A reflective, genial humorist, he was an expert at putting proverbial wisdom into an amusing form and at provoking his audience into the spectacle. His hatred of the nouveaux riches and the philistines, who formed the majority of his audience during the inflation period, often lashed him into improvisations more pointed than his usual humanist tone. On one occasion he remarked to such a group sitting at the front of the cabaret: 'My dear ladies and gentlemen, there in the front. It is bad enough that I have to see you eat in such a time, but also to have to *hear* you eat . . .!

Known as a film actor and script writer, Grünbaum, conférence apart, also produced a variety of short cabaret sketches. One of these, 'The Vote', is an example of his political satire. A dozen worthy men in frock coats stand on a stage devoid of decor. In front of them, an unmistakable figure with toothbrush moustache, speechifies: 'Party members, we are coming to a decision over the important issue of authorization for full emergency powers. Those for, stand up. Those against, sit down.' The gentlemen in frock coats look around searchingly and, since there are no seats, remain standing. Short pause. Then the figure of the Führer states loudly: 'Party members, the motion is unanimously accepted.' The Nazi's claim to dictatorial power by 'democratic' means stands exposed.

Such sketches did not exactly endear Grünbaum to the Nazis and their brutal retaliation during his internment at Dachau resulted in his death in 1939.

Paul Nikolaus was a conférencier with a different style. Acidly satirical, Nikolaus felt that the role of the conférencier was to be less of a humorist than an investigator of contemporary reality. Indeed, his cabaret commentaries were a gloss on the reactionary events of Weimar. Every evening Nikolaus would have the next day's papers, still wet, rushed to him by a press contact. His conférence would then consist of a critical exposé of the news. Hounded by the Nazis, he fled to Zurich in 1933 where a month later he committed suicide. In his final letter to his friends, he invoked them, in his usual witty tone, to 'laugh when you think of me: that is the best form of piety'.

Die Katakombe

Another famous conférencier of the period was Werner Finck, who had a shy, modest style which endeared him to his public. Finck would appear partially hidden behind the stage curtain to deliver his conférence; and so great was his natural comic talent, that without needing to say anything, he sent his audience into peals of laughter. Finck was already well known in cabaret circles when he opened his own locale, Die Katakombe, with the actor Hans Deppe in 1929.

The last four years of the Weimar Republic were rife with cabarets. Some were purely amusement dives or strip clubs. Others, including student cabarets, were revolutionary in intent and mixed agitprop, even street theatre, with a more traditional programme. These latter cabarets were to some extent a product of the radical politicization which had ensued from the Depression. The Katakombe emerges from these into the annals of history, not only because of the excellence of its programme, but because it continued the line of genuinely satirical and politically unaffiliated cabarets. Though some of its performers, like Ernst Busch, might be committed revolutionaries, the Katakombe's tone was never propagandist. Rather, it emphasized the battle against the increasing power of the National Socialists and their apocalyptic ideology of racial purity, and exposed the nature of internment camp existence, along with other aspects of Nazi terror.

Stage Designs for the *Katakombe* by Wolfgang Roth. Courtesy Wolfgang Roth.

In contrast to the poshness of the KadeKo, the Katakombe functioned from a small cellar-like space equipped with wooden tables and chairs, and used a 'poor' stage and improvised costumes. It was the excellence of the material, the troupe's gift for literary parody and social satire, as well as Finck's unique personality, which won a wide audience for the cabaret. On the opening night Finck explained to his public why Katakombe had been chosen as a name: 'Two thousand years ago, the catacombs provided a place of refuge for the first Christians; today it is a place of refuge for the last.'

Quite by chance, Finck recounts in his memoirs, the Katakombe was one of the only cabarets whose performers were completely 'Aryan'. Yet provocation was frequent, for the floor was often filled with Nazis and their informers. On one occasion one of these shouted loudly up to Finck, 'Dirty Jew!' Finck, with his mastery of repartee, calmly answered: 'I'm afraid you're mistaken. I only look this intelligent ...' Despite such quips and the evident anti-Nazi stand of the cabaret, it was not shut down until 1935. In the meantime Finck developed an increasing skill for veiled critique. Due to ingenious verbal play, the content of his statements could never be directly labelled as subversive, though in effect it was. For example, one of the Katakombe sketches pointed out that since a front for German culture had been established, the cabaret could permit itself to form a front for 'Salutary German Humour', the *Kampfbund für den Deutschen heilsamen Humor*, or KfDHH. The final two initials, it was emphasized, did not stand for an abbreviation of the traditional German greeting, Heil Hitler! Nor did they mean ha ha.

When Nazi informers interfered Finck turned to them and said, 'Gentlemen, am I speaking too quickly? Are you following me? Or shall I follow you?' The regime could not permit such satirical attacks to continue for too long, and in May 1935 the cabaret was closed down. The Nazi paper, the *Völkischer Beobachter* noted the reasons for the shut-down in the following way: 'For example, they linked prostitution with the activity of collecting for the *Winterhilfswerk*,¹ and aroused general opposition against collections. They mocked military and party uniforms, ridiculed the organization of the Party, and dragged the national service through the mud. A racially pure Jew, who as such enjoys in Germany only a "guest's" status, dares to make critical remarks on political events in Germany. Consequently the audience mainly consists of Jews and other elements destructive to the state.' The notice terminated in cynical Goebbels jargon. These people were being given the opportunity to make up for their all too lengthy waste of time by being sent to do respectable and solid work in a camp.

Finck, unlike many, survived the ordeal and after the war he returned to the cabaret.

---

¹ A Nazi charity organization, allegedly to help the homeless, which in fact collected funds for military purposes.

Cabaret in Exile

The Third Reich's repressive measures made it impossible for public satirical activity to continue within Germany. As the enemies of the Nazi regime fled to other countries, exile cabarets began to spring up: Vienna, Prague, Zurich, Paris, London. From these centres, writers, actors, composers, set-designers, in a profusion of exiled talent continued the battle against Nazism and exposed its horrors to foreigners who were rarely fully aware of Germany's plight.

It is this harsh period which places the cabaret's artistic and political value into stark relief. In Vienna, for example, while the large and state theatres were increasingly subject to government pressure which, together with shortage of funds, restricted the kind and quality of their programme, the cabaret, with its small, 'poor' stage could still permit the voices of resistance to be heard. Similarly, as newspapers became more and more mouthpieces of reaction, the cabaret still provided a public platform from which events could be 'truthfully' chronicled.

The cabaret's basic features – immediacy and topicality – were well suited to a time when artistic commitment was essential, and writers could as little afford the delay involved in publishing manuscripts, as publishers could afford the cost of printing and distributing books. Although historically there was only a very short time gap between Nazi repression of large-scale cultural enterprises and the small stage, the cabaret's slightly higher threshold of resistance can provide a model for our own time of recession.

Along with the fact that its smallness is to a certain extent the mark of its independence, the cabaret has other intrinsic qualities which make it a perfect medium for hard times. The live contacts between artists and public inherent in the form permits a continuity of artistic activity, innovation, and community. The performer's ability to contradict or give additional nuance to verbal utterance by gesture enables criticism, satire, or simply laughter to emerge where it would otherwise be impossible, such as in print. Finally the improvisational quality of cabaret, which allows constant shifts in content so that an immediate commentary on events is possible; its openness to amateurs; its adaptability to various physical as well as moral climates, makes it a unique art form for survivors. Thus, from 1935 to 1945, manifestations of cabaret could be found in such improbable places as a Canadian internment camp for German and Italian prisoners of war, and in Dachau.

Opposite
Hitler as an open mouth. This is the picture, *Jugend* suggested in 1928, that Stresemann brought home with him from Munich. The cartoon undermines Hitler's seriousness as a political figure, while poking fun at his artistic pretensions. 1928.

Vienna

With the influx of German refugees, Vienna became a centre of political and literary cabaret in the thirties. As early as 1931 the actress Stella Kadmon had founded a cabaret based on the model of the Katakombe and called Der Liebe Augustin. Here the more customary Viennese mixture of whimsy and genial wit was replaced with biting satire, parody, and topical critique. Austria's problematic political and cultural relationship to Germany, its burgeoning right wing, and the Dolfuss dictatorship all became subjects for the cabaret stage.

Then came Die Stachelbeere (Gooseberry), run by Rudolph Spitz, now a London resident, and the famous Literatur am Naschmarkt. This latter cabaret developed a form which mingled the Viennese popular theatre tradition with the political satire and variety of the German cabaret. About forty minutes of the Literatur programme were devoted to a play, and before and after this central piece there were songs, a conférence and sketches. The Literatur's theatrical productions ranged from Nestroy and Thornton Wilder to recreations of old Viennese farces, and original dramas or satires by writers affiliated with the group. The range of the cabaret's programme and the quality and variety of its experimentation still makes it one of the most interesting small stages in theatrical history. In Jura Soyfer this cabaret brought to light a singular dramatic talent: a writer who could use the old Viennese form of the magical farce and infuse it both with a personal poetry and a topical social critique which made him an early victim of the Nazis. In 1938, when Hitler marched into Vienna, the Literatur was playing what was to be its final programme, aptly entitled, *The Viennese goes Under*.

A sketch at the Cornichon. Klaus Budzinski Archiv.

162

Zurich

Like Vienna, Zurich too became a centre for two important anti-Nazi cabarets in the thirties. The first of these, the Pfeffermühle, was initiated by Erika Mann in Munich in 1933 and received its name from her father, Thomas Mann. Together with her brother Klaus, Erika Mann wrote texts, conférences and chansons strongly critical of the Nazis. A few months later, when the threat of imprisonment was near, the Pfeffermühle troupe emigrated to Zurich where they opened their cabaret not far from the site of the old Cabaret Voltaire. Dressed in male garb, Erika Mann acted as conférencière. Her quick-witted imaginative presentation, together with Thérèse Giese's acting and singing ability, made the cabaret an overnight success.

Despite its proclaimed 'neutrality', Switzerland's policy at that time was to do nothing to anger the Nazi regime. Thus the Pfeffermühle, with its overt anti-Nazi politics, was not only severely criticized by the press, but directly assaulted. Nazi supporters arrived *en masse* to break up the programmes, launched stink bombs, and on one occasion there was an actual bomb scare. While police searched the premises Erika Mann calmly continued to improvise a conférence. Finally the Zurich canton passed a 'Lex Pfeffermühle', which prohibited foreigners from appearing on stage in any programme which had political content. The cabaret's Zurich term was at an end, but before the group disbanded it carried its satire to the rest of Switzerland, Holland, Belgium, Luxemburg and Czechoslovakia, giving a total of 1034 performances.

What the troupe left to Zurich was a tradition of political cabaret. By the end of 1934 the city had its own anti-fascist cabaret which launched an assault against potential dictatorship in Switzerland. Calling itself the Cornichon, this cabaret drew on native talent. It used the local Swiss German, and developed a programme so successful that it outlasted the war.

Above
Erika Mann acting as conférencière at the *Pfeffermühle*. Klaus Budzinski Archiv.

Left
Therese Giese at the *Pfeffermühle*. Klaus Budzinski Archiv.

163

London

The cabaret form had never really taken hold in England, either as a meeting and performance place for writers and artists, or as a centre for satirical dissent. The reasons for this remain speculative. In comparison to the continent, institutions in England are genuinely more democratic, and to a certain extent this defuses socio-political satire of the more acid and ideological sort. Then too, given that the major English newspapers were on the whole 'information-givers' not obviously in the pay of reactionary forces, critics are less driven to underground forms of protest. In its German political variety Kabarett is a surrogate for journalism, and is in many ways an extreme form intended for fighting extremes.

The English stage before the war was either dedicated to full-scale theatre or to music hall. While the latter had of course its share of slapstick humour, any acid social criticism or political satire were purely accidental to its nature, as indeed was artistic innovation. Nor did serious intellectuals or writers look upon this medium as a possible vehicle for their own work. As for the theatre proper (pace Wilde, Shaw and Gilbert and Sullivan), its wit was not directly calculated to move any spectator out of comfortable complacency; while popular pub entertainment – the closest equivalent in terms of setting to European cabaret – was rarely metamorphosed into anything more than entertainment. Such too was the case with revues of the Fargeon variety and with the night-club. The Café de Paris, the inter-war period's most star-studded locale, found its best satirist in Noel Coward, who is closest in style and in chanson-writing talent to a French or German cabaretist. Yet Coward himself is in the final appraisal a brittle rather than a critical wit, socialite rather than socialist. And despite the presence of such brilliant performers as Beatrice Lillie and Eartha Kitt, the Café de Paris lacked that mixture of social and political satire, artistic innovation, and entertainment which is the essence of genuine cabaret. Then too, the Café de Paris catered to the moneyed élite, and not to the general public or, like a centre for experimentation and artistic exchange, to an intimate circle of artists. It is not a coincidence that the antiquated British stage censorship was never seriously challenged between the end of World War I and the sixties.

Another possible reason for the lack of cabaret in England until the sixties boom in satire lies in the fact that the English cultural climate differs from the continental in not being prone to avant-garde movements which self-consciously define themselves as such, whether artistically or in terms of political engagement. It is not surprising that when such a movement did arise before World War I, around Wyndham Lewis, it found its meeting place in a French-style cabaret, The Cave of the Golden Calf. Decorated by Gill, Lewis and Gore, the cabaret gave theatrical performances and was designed to 'promote a desirable intimacy between all artistic classes' and to 'provide throughout the night a refuge place, an atmosphere of vivid colours, music, and motion'. However, in the thirties, when the vanguard of English poetry did define itself in terms of political engagement, then the means of furthering consciousness and commitment was not generally a performance style which mixed popular appeal with a serious satirical intent. On the whole 'cabaret' in England still popularly designates an intimate strip club or form of 'show' where song and music provide the trimmings for varying degrees of provocative nudity.

In 1939, however, and throughout the war, London was the centre of fully fledged continental cabaret. It came with German and Austrian refugees and played for several years both to members of the émigré community and, once English had been mastered, to the public at large. The cabaretists' purpose was severalfold: to maintain morale among the refugees, who had not only to acclimatize themselves to foreign habits but to undergo the difficulties of alien registration and internment camps; to continue the battle against fascism; and to give a largely uninformed English public an inkling of the day-to-day human reality behind Hitler's propaganda speeches. The means were the witty chanson, acid political satire, and a 'poor' stage used effectively by ingenious designers.

Martin Miller, on the left, in a scene from *The Good Soldier Schweik*. Courtesy Hannah Norbert.

The Lantern troupe in *No Orchids for Mr Hitler*. Courtesy Hannah Norbert.

The Lantern

The first exile cabaret in London was created by Austrian refugees. Its name suggests its nature: The Lantern, an exiled cousin of Karl Kraus's piercingly satirical review, *The Torch*. Composed mostly of notable Austrian stage figures, such as Marianne Walla, Fritz Schrecker and Hannah Norbert, the group had as its producer-director the versatile actor Martin Miller, and numbered among its writers Rudolf Spitz and Hugo Königsgarten. Nearly all adepts of the Viennese *Kleinkunstbühne*, the group introduced this cabaretistic form to England. Working first of all from a tiny improvised stage in Westbourne Terrace and then from Hampstead, the Viennese Theatre Club, as they were known, put on topical satirical revues as well as plays such as *The Good Soldier Schweik* and *Volpone*. The group provided a satirical commentary on Vienna under Nazi rule in a series of quick-moving sketches, complete with chansons and brilliantly improvised sets. They transmuted Wagner's *Rheingold* characters into Hitler and his henchmen (singing, of course); portrayed the fate of refugee aliens at registration offices; and enacted literary 'travesties' or parodies. The revue titles speak for themselves: *On the Way*, *From Adam to Adolf*, *No Orchids for Mr Hitler*, *Here is the News*.

One of the Lantern's sketches practically produced an international incident. In the second of the group's programmes Martin Miller performed a Hitler parody entitled 'The Führer Speaks', in which he reproduced minutely all the peculiarities of Hitler's diction and gesture. On April Fools' Day 1940, the BBC broadcast Miller's performance.

Party Members, men and women of the German Reich Convention, when in 1492 the Spaniard Columbus undertook his now well-known journey over the distant ocean, using German-made instruments and the results of German science, there could have been no doubt that with the success of this daring enterprise, Germany had to have some part in the achievement which this voyage of discovery was to result in . . .

166

'The Führer speaks.' Martin Miller as a bogus Hitler at the Lantern. Courtesy Hannah Norbert.

Ever since 1492 I have remained silent and left this problem untouched in the interests of peace. But now my patience is at an end.

(There follows a recapitulation of Hitler's heroic and self-sacrificing rise to power and a summary of recent 'protective' politics.)

I hereby firmly declare that I have now made my last territorial demands in Europe, but beyond that I have now to state certain claims of a maritime nature . . . There are in America national minorities closely connected by race and tradition with the German Reich. In Chicago alone, there are 324,000 Czechs, and they keep asking themselves, 'Why can't we come under the Protectorate?' In the well-known city of New York, there are 476,000 Poles . . . They have a right to be protected by Germany and I shall enforce that right . . .

Miller's sentence structure, the rhythm of his speech, and his intonations were unmistakably Hitler's. And the parodied speech was interspersed with the relevant 'bravos' 'heils' and 'pfuis'. Shades of Orson Welles's *War of the Worlds*. A somewhat panicky CBS immediately contacted the BBC to discover where this latest Hitler broadcast, which they seemed to have missed, had come from. They were not the only ones to fall into the trap of Miller's bogus Hitler.

167

Four and Twenty Black Sheep and the Little Theatre

By July 1939 German refugees, among them photomonteur John Heartfield and the writers Egon Larsen and Frederick Gotfurt, had organized themselves into a theatre collective which, though its members gradually exceeded the number, called itself *Four and Twenty Black Sheep*. In the West End Arts Theatre, they staged a cabaret revue, *Going, Going -Gong!* which continued the satirical battle against Nazism. Topical sketches were written by various members of the collective and songs and poems by Brecht, Mehring, and Ringelnatz were added to these.

Although the revue was a success, the collective found itself severely in deficit. It disbanded, but many of its members, under the leadership of Erich Freund and Frederick Gotfurt, then became part of the Little Theatre, a group subsidized by the Free German League of Culture. Throughout the war years the group put on political satirical revues, which in many instances provided a more piercing view of events than the newspapers themselves.

The opening song of the 1940 revue, *What's in the News?*, was called 'Stop Press' and it provides some idea of the group's handling of a mixed German-English idiom, as well as of the nature of their satire.

First reader: *Was bringt die Zeitung?*
                  Nichts von Bedeutung.
                  In Hampstead hat ein Hund gebellt,
                  Es gibt nichts Neues auf der Welt.

                  What's in the papers?
                  Nothing significant.
                  In Hampstead a dog barked,
                  There's nothing new in the world.

Second reader: My paper makes me soon forget
                  This world of hate and hustle.
                  I take it with me in my bed . . .
                  And do the crossword puzzle!

In the same revue a sixteen-year-old, Agnes Bernell, who was to emerge as one of the group's top actresses, sang 'The Twenty-Year-Old Cosmopolite', by Egon Larsen and Frederick Gotfurt. The song portrays the baffling trajectory of the refugees and their plight:

                  Je connais tout le quartier
                  Et au Montmartre les cabarets.
                  Paris est belle quand on est riche.
                  Mais comme une refugiée – je m'en fiche.

                  In Kuba liess man uns nicht landen.
                  In Spanien fühlt ich mich zuhaus.
                  Mich fischte, als die Mine krachte,
                  ein netter Matrose heraus.

                  Ich kenn' die Welt. Sie lässt mich kalt.

Agnes Bernell in *What's in the News?* 'The Twenty-Year Old Cosmopolite'. Courtesy Egon Larsen.

168

Mr Gulliver goes to School, 'Never Say Lie'.
Courtesy Egon Larsen.

Ich bin schon ganze zwanzig Jahre alt.

Vom Reisen träumt ich als Kind,
Von Abenteuren, Seefahrt und Wind.
Jetzt ist's ein Haus, von dem ich oft träum',
Und eine Stadt; sie heisst daheim.

Ich möcht' sie einmal wiedersehen
Und hör'n wie man Deutsch spricht zuhaus.
Ich könnt dort die Menschen verstehen,
ist alles das erst einmal aus.

Ich kenn' die Welt. Sie ist so kalt.
Ich bin schon ganze zwanzig Jahre alt.

This region is familiar to me.
So are Montmartre's cabarets to me.
When one's rich, Paris is just grand.
As a refugee, it's not worth a damn.

In Cuba they wouldn't let us land.
Spain felt like home, or just about.
When the mine exploded in the sand,
A handsome sailor fished me out.

I know the world. It leaves me cold.
I'm now all of twenty years old.

As a child, travel was my dream.
On windy seas, I longed to roam.
Now there's one spot of which I dream,
One city, and that's called home.

I wish I could see it once again,
Hear how German sounds from where I stem,
Understand when I'm being addressed . . .
But that's all over now, I guess.

I know the world. It is so cold.
I'm now all of twenty years old.

Mr Gulliver Goes to School was another of the group's collectively devised revues. Gulliver's educational adventure here consisted in
meeting with a contemporary variety of dwarfs and giants: the Master
Race, Hampstead's continental inhabitants, officials in a citizen's

169

advice bureau and farmers in Hitler's Germany. The group's various satirical targets were linked by Gulliver's comments, who cast an imminently reasonable eye on topical instances of gross unreason.

In 1944 the group put on *My Goodness, My Alibi*, an ironic prophecy of what were to be the Nuremberg trials. This featured Sherlock Holmes in twenty songs and scenes producing evidence against a variety of 'enemies of the people', ranging from the archetypal escapist on his desert island to Nietzsche. This was, of course, only after Mussolini, Hitler and other VIP's had been tried by the international court of the people.

The English stage would only see the equivalent of this kind of political cabaret again some twenty years later.

'Back to Paradise' from *My Goodness, My Alibi*. Courtesy Egon Larsen.

Life and After-Life

Three decades have now almost passed since Europe woke to the ravages left by total war. The intervening years have seen such problems as the Cold War and the Bomb, American policy in Vietnam, the Biafra crisis, racism, child battery and sexual hypocrisy attacked from the locus of cabaret stages throughout the world. Cabarets have sprung up, shut their doors or had them forcibly shut by authority, in Europe both east and west, and in America. The cabaret form itself has been dismembered into its component parts to become a segment of our heritage through television and the mass distribution of records. *Diseuses*, like Edith Piaf, have brought the 'existential' chanson into every home, just as Jacques Brel, Georges Brassens and Tom Lehrer have done for the satirical song, and Bob Dylan and the East German Wolf Biermann for the satirical-protest song.

So too, with the Americans Mort Sahl, Dick Gregory and Lenny Bruce and the Austrian Helmut Qualtinger, the cabaret conférence, ranging in tone from mild wit to confessional virulence, has become either one part of a variety programme or the principal focus of one-man shows. Fringe theatres have adopted the intimacy of cabaret, its audience provocation tactics and its improvisational ambience. And Humpty-Dumpty like, all the elements of cabaret have been put back together again in cabaret satirical revues like England's *Beyond the Fringe* and Peter Brook's *US*, in television cabaret, or in nostalgic re-creations like the musical and film *Cabaret*.

Most recently, the recessionary eighties have witnessed a revival of artistic and satirical cabaret both in Britain and the USA. From London's Comic Strip to the Cabaret Futura, from the quick-fire grotesqueries of Alexei Sayle to the wild and furious rock, dance and mixed media performances of Richard Strange, and across the Atlantic to Manhattan's heady Danceteria and Mudd Club, cabaret lives with an energy as eclectic and innovatory as to delight The Black Cat of its ancestry.

Post-war Germany

In the years just after the war, when a divided Germany was attempting to come to terms with its devastation and develop a peace-time policy, many former cabaret figures returned to the small stage. Valeska Gert, back from America, tirelessly attempted to provide

Helmut Qualtinger in one of his acts. Courtesy Photo Hoffenreich.

satire and entertainment in the ruins of what had once been Berlin. Willy Schäffer, the conférencier, reopened the Kabarett der Komiker, and in Munich Werner Finck formed a cabaret collective called Das Schmunzelkolleg, Laughter lectures, while Erich Kästner cooperated in establishing first *Die Schaubude*, and then *Die Kleine Freiheit*.

One emphasis of the post-war cabaret was a critique of Adenauer's restrictive politics and a desire for the establishment of social democracy. To this the cabarets added a serio-comic analysis of the 'national characteristics' which had permitted the rise of Nazism and the atrocities of war to take place. Finally, in a time which desperately called for humour and irony, the cabaret provided what Finck's group named 'a school for laughter'.

But as the fifties grew more affluent and turned into the sixties, and the Berlin Wall rose up to become a material symbol of the world's bifurcation, the German cabaret's laughter became ever grimmer. Black humour was already evident in Helmut Qualtinger, Vienna's foremost cabaret figure of the period. Corpulent to circus dimensions, Qualtinger is a brilliant satirist and performer who emerged as the Austrian personification of the angry young man. His one-man play, *Herr Karl*, first staged in 1961 was the final possible word on the Viennese 'Little man'. Subtly performed in Viennese dialect by Qualtinger, Herr Karl, through various scenes and confrontations, appears as a shabby, shuffling opportunist who arranges his ideas to fit whatever the dominant political colour. Hypocritical and corrupt to the core, Herr Karl was the living condemnation of Viennese *Schlamperei*; a virulent attack on the state of mind which had accepted Nazi rule and might bend to any other. But Qualtinger's *Herr Karl*, bitter as it might be, was still a masterful piece of satire, something which the sixties cabaretists in Germany generally eschewed for the sake of didacticism and agitation.

This new generation of cabaretists was for the most part composed of the immediate forerunners of the international student protest movement. Being polemically aggressive and members of the radical new left who wished to form a non-parliamentary opposition, these cabaretists refused on the whole to provide 'consumer entertainment'. They had watched an older group of satirists being assimilated by the mass market of television, their criticism taken in painlessly as an entertaining commodity. And so they produced 'anti-cabaret', deliberately undermining the cabaret's built-in entertainment factor. 'Beware', the title of one of their programmes claimed, 'The mandolin is loaded!'

Laughter which arose out of witty satire was understood by this young new left as a way of adapting to the status quo. Once a problem had been laughed at, the very activity of laughter replaced any urgent need for activity on a more constructive level. The basis of this analysis has an ancient, if diametrically opposed, parallel. The Greeks had created satyr plays partially in order to distract the gods by laughter – for while they were thus distracted, they could not give vent to their destructive force. In both cases, laughter is seen to be a suspension of activity. The aim of these new cabaretists was to illuminate the contemporary situation and raise consciousness about socialism. As it had been for the satirists of the twenties, the cabaret stage was only one platform for their activity, which would find its culmination in radical social change.

Of the many sixties cabarets which fall into this general category, the most notable are perhaps Hannelore Kaub's Bügelbrett, a student collective, Floh de Cologne, and Berlin's Reichskabarett. But this political development in German cabaret is best typified by the writer-performer Wolfgang Neuss, who also appears as its most incisive satirist. Neuss began his cabaretistic activity as a critic of the status quo and a supporter of the then oppositional Social Democrats. His fame reached national proportions when in 1965 he put on a one-man show, the *Neuss Testament*, which was an adaptation of Villon's testament to suit contemporary personalities and conditions. Neuss also sporadically published a newspaper called *Neuss Deutschland*, German Neuss-paper, in parody of the East German Neues or New Deutschland. This earned him the reputation of being a *Linksaussenseiter*, a left-outfielder, an acceptable critical position. In 1968, however, when, like many young socialists, Neuss attacked the Social Democrat's policies within an essentially right-of-centre coalition which did not defy American intervention in Vietnam, he began to be hounded by the press. His satire directed against Berlin's 'neo-fascist fever' and the Social Democrat's betrayal of socialism became increasingly bitter. Finally, his disgust with his own country led to temporary withdrawal to Sweden. Ironically, the East German singer-satirist, Wolf Biermann, was simultaneously singing his vehement critique of his Germany's failure to achieve revolutionary socialism and the mockery it made of 'freedom'.

While many of Germany's sixties cabarets based their critique of society on a Marxist analysis and propagated revolutionary politics, their programmes dealt as often with immediate social issues as with polemics. The tactic, as Munich's Rationaltheater exemplifies, is to begin with a pressing topical problem, analyse it and trace it implacably down to its source. In the process clichéd assumptions and perspectives are undermined and the whole of a given social system is seen to be problematic. What emerges is Documentary Cabaret, a mixture of sung statistics, monologues and sketches which bear the marks of in-depth investigation, film, photographs and music all tellingly juxtaposed to climax in a total social critique.

America

While the German cabaret in the sixties was becoming increasingly polemical, anatomizing capitalism and insisting on the necessity for revolutionary upheaval, England and America were experiencing a stage satire boom of a kind unseen since the eighteenth century. As they were produced by societies which were never as theoretical in their political orientation as those of the continent, these Anglo-American cabaretists could still point their barbs at the traditional targets of satire: pedantic dogmatism, fossilized beliefs and life styles — all those institutions, political forms, moral or philosophical systems which, together with their standard-bearers, function as if their abstract principles were more significant than people and their experience. Compared to their continental peers they were traditional, but these cabaretists were unique in their own environment. For it was the first time, since the birth of cabaret, that English and American satirists were to launch a full-scale assault on their societies and their ruling powers from the position of the small stage.

If one is to enter the heady area of origins, it all began with the beat scene in America. The beats were living out a protest against accepted American values; the restrictive, materialistic, clean-cut, upright and up-tight values of a white suburban middle class, of which McCarthy was the ideologue as Eisenhower was the representative. The main means of protest was to adopt a life-style diametrically opposed to that of the American bourgeoisie. Like the bohemians of Bruant's day, they identified themselves with vagrants and underdogs, took on dress and a manner which was aggressively 'un-American', propagated a more open and less hypocritical form of sexuality, and insisted on the 'existential' and artistic value of experience, rather than on material ends and ambition. And just as the avant-garde had done after World War I, the beats adopted jazz as their 'sound', the music of the blacks whose style incorporated all facets of the beat protest against middle-class America. Ironically, it was through this first stay-at-home bohemia that jazz finally came home to America.

Small clubs began to spring up in the major American cities, meeting places for the beats where jazz could be heard. In one of these, San Francisco's hungry i, beat poetry was read, sometimes in jazz-poetry duets, sometimes on its own. Except for the lack of a political outlook and socio-political satire, a structural comparison could be drawn with the New Objectivists of the German twenties and their Kabaretts. Then in 1953, enter Mort Sahl, America's first political wit and conférencier, or, as American idiom would have it, hip monologuist and stand-up comedian. For the next decade American cabaret flourished under the aegis of the 'Sickniks', Mort Sahl, Shelley Berman, the sketch-team Mike Nichols and Elaine May, and the inimitable Lenny Bruce, 'America's Number 1 Vomic' as he was dubbed by a leading columnist.

Several features distinguish these figures from the more traditional American nightclub comics such as Bob Hope, and make them stand out as genuine satirical cabaretists. All of them wrote their own routines and did not rely on professional 'comic' writers. They adopted a casual manner on stage, acting as if the stage did not exist and speaking directly to their audience. Their attitude to this audience was half intimate, half hostile, for like the original cabaretists they were breaking down the mystique of the stage and simultaneously provoking or insulting their audience into reaction or participation. Finally they broke the political taboo and deliberately engaged in topical political satire, something no American performer had dared to do on the small stage, despite the laxity of American libel laws.

174

By the sheer outlandishness of their quips and the daring vituperative quality of their monologues, they rose beyond entertainment and professionalism into the area of satirical art.

The American sickniks bared their fangs and concentrated on tearing apart the hypocritical sentimentalities and prejudices implicit in conventional attitudes and roles. For maximum effect, they used shock tactics on their audience, told sick, outrageous tales in a language which was a mixture of ghetto, hip, jazz and psychoanalytical talk, and Yiddish. Here is how *Time* magazine, in its unique prose, summarized these sickniks: 'They joked about father and Freud; about mother and masochism; about sister and sadism. They delightedly told of airline pilots throwing out a few passengers to lighten the load, of a graduate school for dope addicts, of parents so loving they always "got upset if anyone else made me cry". They attacked motherhood, childhood, sainthood, and in perhaps a dozen nightclubs across the country – from Manhatten's Den to Chicago's Mr Kelly's to San Francisco's hungry i – audiences paid stiff prices to soak it up.'

Mort Sahl, the first of America's political cabaretists, prepared his haranguing monologues in true conférencier fashion by scanning the day's newspapers, magazines, and radio broadcasts. He aimed his barbs at the mating and sexual habits of the fifties young, at their apathy and cynicism. Improvising much of his material and shooting it out in machine-gun staccato, he began his first performance at the hungry i in 1953, with the suggestion that someone might be moved to invent a new kind of Eisenhower jacket to be called a McCarthy jacket, its distinguishing feature being an extra zipper to go over the mouth. He continued to quip, 'for a while every time the Russians threw an American in jail, the Un-American Activities Committee would retaliate by throwing an American in jail too'. Cold warriorism, the hate hysteria of the McCarthy era, had never been challenged in this way from the stage before, and Sahl was a sensation. So much of a national sensation that some seven years later in 1960 *Time* magazine printed 'A Sahl's Eye-View of the Unfabulous Fifties', and used such satirical tidbits as:

On Ike's (Eisenhower's) first election: 'We need a man on a white horse. Well we got the horse, but there's nobody on him.'

On Nixon in Russia: 'If he doesn't get along with them, he'll be in trouble, because over there he can't call anyone a Communist and hurt their career.'

On the Missile Gap: 'Maybe the Russians will steal all our secrets. Then they'll be two years behind.'

Nichols and May were a famous satirical team who examined America's doctors and performed their own brand of incisive psychoanalysis on its neurotics. They originated from University of Chicago student theatre groups which had established The Second City. This group like the later Committee in San Francisco, wrote their programmes collectively and aimed their poisonous arrows at bigoted governers of southern states as well as at the foibles of intellectuals and the

Mike Nichols and Elaine May. Library of the Performing Arts, New York.

175

middle class. The Nichols and May team were also adepts at literary parody and on request would do sketches simulating the styles of anyone from Clifford Odets to Joyce to Pirandello. Greenwich Village was heir to The Second City group and when Nichols and May split up – the first becoming an acclaimed film director – Elaine May established a second Village cabaret, The Premise. Both these locales were to serve as satirical centres of the early sixties, and one of their favourite targets was Nixon: Richard Nixon came down to breakfast wearing his new liberal mask. His daughter reacted with a scream. 'Momma – who's that man?'

Political cabaret did have one important precedent in America. In the thirties during the days of the government-funded Federal Theatre, The Living Newspaper had been set up as an attempt to unite political theatre with popular entertainment. This project was run along the lines of a large newspaper, with a general editor and reporters covering various areas, with the aim of providing contemporary political commentary in a fashion which would appeal to large numbers of people. Elements of circus, variety show, ballet, film projection and music were used in cabaret revue manner. But The Living Newspaper started off with a programme which dealt with the Ethiopian crisis and immediately there were government protests – no critique of foreign politicians or major figures was to be made from a federally financed stage. The Living Newspaper then turned its gaze to America's internal situation, only to find vicious right-wing reaction growing on all sides. Programmes on left-wing politics were to be its death. This short-lived project was much more theatrically ambitious and politically critical than the fifties and sixties cabaretists, yet one of these latter was to be hounded into near martyrdom by similar forces of reaction.

Lenny Bruce's artistic trajectory has become something of a legend, starting as a strip-club MC through a slew of obscenity trials, to one-man show in New York's Carnegie Hall and finally to suicide by drug overdose. For Bruce lived out the archetype of America's underground man, an amoral iconoclast who flourished in the hipster subculture of sex, jazz and junk. Bruce's outspoken, haranguing monologues, with their mixture of satire and obsessional confession, were the most virulent of the period. They are known in show-biz idiom as the 'Spritz': a fast, freely associative rush of words, spiced with ghetto idiom, simulating jazz, and pushing further and further into the realms of the outlandishly unorthodox until new satirical and comic insights are reached.

Spilling over with words, Bruce unleashed his venom on the fetishes of liberal piety, on sexual hypocrisy, racism, the bomb, organized religion and on America's greed for profit. An acute observer and mimic of gesture and voice, he would puncture his own monologues with a word from the omnipresent American sponsor: 'Hello out there. Are you tired and run down? Do you lack the strength to throw that rope up over a limb and put in a full day of lynching? If so, try high-potency Lynch-em-ell. And now, back to our film . . .' So it went in the days of the freedom marchers.

Here is an extract of Lenny Bruce, unforgettable Yiddishisms and all, exploding racial and religious clichés, concerned with his own people, the Jews, and going on to touch on much more than that:

I always try to search out the meaning of any clichés that attach to any ethnic group. And I've always heard that stupid *bubeh miseh* [old wive's tale] about Jews and all the smut books, and all. But here's where all that must come from – and in part it's true. Dig. . . . There's no word in Yiddish that describes oral copulation. In fact, there are no gutter phrases in Yiddish – it's amazing. Homosexuality is known as 'the English disease'. *Emmis* [really]. There are no words in Jewish that describe any sexual act – *emmis* – or parts, or lusts . . .

To a Jew f-u-c-k and s-h-i-t have the same value on the dirty word graph. A Jew has no concept that f-u-c-k is worth 90 points, and s-h-i-t 10. And the reason for that is that – well, see, rabbis and priests both s-h-i-t, but only one f-u-c-ks.

You see, in Jewish culture, there's no merit badge for not doing that . . . Now the reason, perhaps, for my irreverence is that I have no knowledge of the god, because the Jews lost their god. Really. Before I was born the god was going away.

Because to have a god you have to know something about him, and as a child, I didn't speak the same language as the Jewish god.

To have a god you have to love him and know about him as kids – early instruction – and I didn't know what he looked like. Our god has no mother, no father, no manger in the five-and-ten, on cereal boxes and on television shows. The Jewish god – what's his face? Moses? Ah, he's a friend of god's:

'I dunno. Moses, he's I dunno, his uncle, I dunno . . .'
He has no true identity. Is he a strong god? Are there little stories? Are there Bible tales about god, that one god, our faceless god?

The Christian god, you're lucky in that way, because you've got Mary, a mother, a father, a beginning, the five-and-ten little mangers – identity. Your god, the Christian god, is all over. He's on rocks, he saves you, he's dying on bank buildings – he's been in three films. He's on crucifixes all over. It's a story you can follow. Constant identification.

The Jewish god – where's the Jewish god? He's on a little box nailed to the door jamb. In a *mezuzah*. There he is, in there. He's standing on a slant, god. And all the Jews are looking at him, and kissing him on the way into the house:

'I told the super (building superintendent) *don't paint god!* Hey super! C'mere. What the hell's the matter with you? I told you twenty times, that's *god* there. What're you painting god for? My old lady kissed the doorbell three times this week. You paint here, here, but don't paint there, alright? Never mind, it's dirty, we'll take care of it. Alright.

'Wait a minute . . . Maybe he's not in there any more . . . maybe the Puerto Ricans stole him – they probably would, to make more garbage. That's it . . . I dunno what to do . . . You wanna open it

Lenny Bruce by David Levine. © Copyright *New York Review-Opera Mundi*.

177

up? . . . Yeah? We'll pry it open, if he's in there . . . *Gevult!* [Blimey!] They stashed a joint!'

Now there's a curtain line for great Jewish theatre. This would be a caper on Broadway. The old Jewish couple, there they are, they open up the *mezuzah*, and the guy goes:

'*Gevult!* They stashed a joint!'

Boom! Curtain.

That's vernacular for a marijuana cigarette. You'd make a bad vice officer, for Chrissake.

Bruce's manner of giving public voice to thoughts and words which generally remain unspoken and unacceptable not only on stage but within the entirety of the liberal establishment created a bombshell. He was playing on the very nerves of his country and making its semi-hidden obsessions — race, sex, puritanism, religion, drugs as stimulants — his own confessed ones. With boundless nihilistic irreverence, he was shooting down gods, heroes, public figures and, even more significantly, was seen by his own time to be violating public assumptions of 'decency' and social codes. The age would not stand for it.

Contemporary verbal permissiveness is in part due to the efforts of performers such as Bruce who demystified a whole range of verbal and conceptual taboos simply by insisting on their public utterence. Through such champions sexuality was released from its puritan hideout in the dark backrooms of pornographers' shops. But in his own time Bruce was hounded by the authorities, who arrested him on drug offences and assiduously taped his performances. He was tried in various states for obscenity, only to emerge from his many battles against censorship as a harassed, if somewhat paranoid, crusader for free speech. He was the embodiment of his time's underground dream of the cool, audacious hipster. He was also to have a marked effect on the English satire of the sixties.

England

In October 1960, returning from a spell in America, Kenneth Tynan launched an appeal in *The Observer* for the establishment of satirical cabaret, which could act as a laboratory, a training ground for satire at large and serve as an incubator of non-conformism. The English theatre, he claimed, had been 'infected and injured' by its weakness in this ancillary department of cabaret:

Where else but in a small room late at night before an audience more notable for its mind than its money, can the true satirist, whether writer or performer or both – practise his art and polish his weapons? In such an atmosphere, he need not restrict himself to the hints and nudges that masquerade as satire in West End revues.

178

He can be outrageous and uninhibited; he can pierce to the quick of the ulcer without bothering to administer sedation; he can speak freely on any subject from the Cuban revolution to the Immaculate Conception . . . Cabaret of this sort is not only satirical in itself, but the cause that satire is in other theatrical forms.

Tynan went on to introduce the American cabaretists to his English public, bemoaning the fact that England had ample clip joints with androgynous floor shows but no 'place where intelligent like-minded people can spend a cheap evening listening to cabaret that is socially, sexually, politically pungent'.

Almost miraculously some eight months later, Tynan's call was answered. Four young men, whose names have now become household words – Jonathan Miller, Alan Bennett, Peter Cook and Dudley Moore – on a May night in 1961 introduced the element of cabaret satire into the dusty, tired, West End revue and threw London into convulsive laughter. The content of *Beyond the Fringe* is now so well known that its original and shocking freshness is difficult to recapture. Here on the stage were four young men looking like four ordinary young men and not rigged up in stage costume, talking about things which people talked about outside the theatre, and, unlike the usual hired puppets of stage illusion, speaking their own words. English stage convention was shattered by the arrival of the cabaret tradition. Contemporary events were being seen on the stage, and accepted proprieties and prejudices spoofed, despite the continuing grip of censorship. Had the Lord Chamberlain's venerable office – in existence without much change for some three hundred years – tripped up in its cobwebs? The story goes that one of the few alterations in the script asked for by the censor was that a stage direction which read 'Enter two outrageous old queens' – be changed to 'Enter two aesthetic young men' – since it was policy not to permit homosexuality to be represented on stage.

The *Beyond the Fringe* group had grown out of university revue and cabaret work. Its humour was whimsical, sometimes zany, sometimes genuinely satirical. And although the satire was mild in comparison to its German predecessor or American relative, it was revolutionary within its own setting. One sketch showed Jonathan Miller as one of the new radical vicars who in the late fifties were bringing rock 'n roll into the churches so as to win larger congregations: 'Now I think an awful lot of tommyrot has been spoken about teenage and juvenile violence, I think we can use this violence and channel it towards God. It is my aim to get the violence off the streets and into the churches where it belongs . . .' The group was irreverent about the establishment, and critical of conservative politics, of English institutions and the unquestioning respect attributed to them, as well as of somewhat phoney progressive trends. Above all, they were brilliantly witty and could spoof linguistic philosophy just as impudently as the perennial stiff-upper-lip, have-another-cup-of-tea Briton. The public seemed to have been waiting just for this, for they lapped it all up and asked for more. The British boom in satire had been launched.

Just as in America, the English satire boom was linked with the protest movement. While the main channel of protest in America was the civil rights movement, in England it found its focus in CND and the Aldermaston marches. In both countries the forms and properties of the so-called establishment were under attack, along with the Cold War politics which they had fathered. In 1961 Macmillan's conservative rule seemed unbudgeable and the stuffiness that it stood for provided a ready-made target for satire. Yet signs of turmoil had been visible ever since that moment in 1956 when John Osborne's *Look Back in Anger* had voiced the disquiet of the young. When the satire boom was at its peak between 1961 and 1963, English society was already well into that permissive heyday which turned certain long-held values topsy-turvy and gained London the reputation in the media of being the swinging world capital of the sixties.

Beyond the Fringe was a revue in cabaret style. It was followed in October 1961 by the opening in Soho of a genuine cabaret, the Establishment. Under the direction of Peter Cook and Nicholas Luard, five thousand people contributed two guineas a piece to provide the funds for the locale. The club environment provided not only intimacy, but also freedom from censorship. Numbering in its regular company John Bird, Jeremy Geidt, John Fortune, Eleanor Bron and Carol Simpson, the Establishment's performance team was increased by visiting performers and by the improvisational talents of the *Beyond the Fringe* group, who appeared for the late post-theatre show. The cabaret was filled to overflowing and for some two years it served as headquarters for the 'bright, new England' — television people, those associated with the equally new colour supplements, pop art, jazz and satire, which had just received a further boost in the launching of the satirical magazine, *Private Eye*.

The Establishment began a vitriolic attack on the whole upper-class charade. Royalty, judges, conservative ministers, all those who sprouted upper class accents were game for their wit. The virulence of the satire is perhaps best understood when one realizes that on the public, that is non-club stage, censorship forbade the presentation or mention of royalty or government figures in any disrespectful light, thereby generally undermining any possibility of political satire. Thus while the only radical theatre of the time, the Royal Court, could never really touch satire, the Establishment was staging a skit which showed Christ as an upper-class gentleman hanging on the cross between two cockney thieves who kept complaining, 'E's gettin all the vinegar sponges!'

Potent though the satire of the Establishment group might be, it was a mere 'pinprick', Kenneth Tynan and Jonathan Miller agreed, to the 'bloodbath' of Lenny Bruce. Bruce, a favourite of the Establishment players, arrived at the club in 1962. The press had already warned the English public of the nature of his wit. Quoting from American papers, who had been shocked by Bruce's routines, they labelled him 'The Man from Outer Taste' and 'A Vulgar Tasteless Boor'. In strong contrast, Tynan, who had attended Bruce's first night together with a select group of initiates, spoke of Bruce as a Yiddish Ariel and suggested that audiences prepare themselves for the performance by going over their Marx and Freud among other selected works.

But not surprisingly, the greater part of the English public who attended Bruce's Establishment evenings found his deeply rooted American idiom totally incomprehensible. Or they picked the more comprehensible aspects of his act – his four letter words and tirades on sexual hypocrisy – out of their context only to find them both shocking and revolting. Despite support from various influential press quarters, Bruce was denied entry on his next trip to England.

If the 'evangelist of the new morality', as George Melly called Bruce, was something of a controversial figure on the English satirical scene,

Jonathan Miller, Dudley Moore, Peter Cook and Alan Bennett, in a scene from *Beyond the Fringe*. Photograph Zoë Dominic.

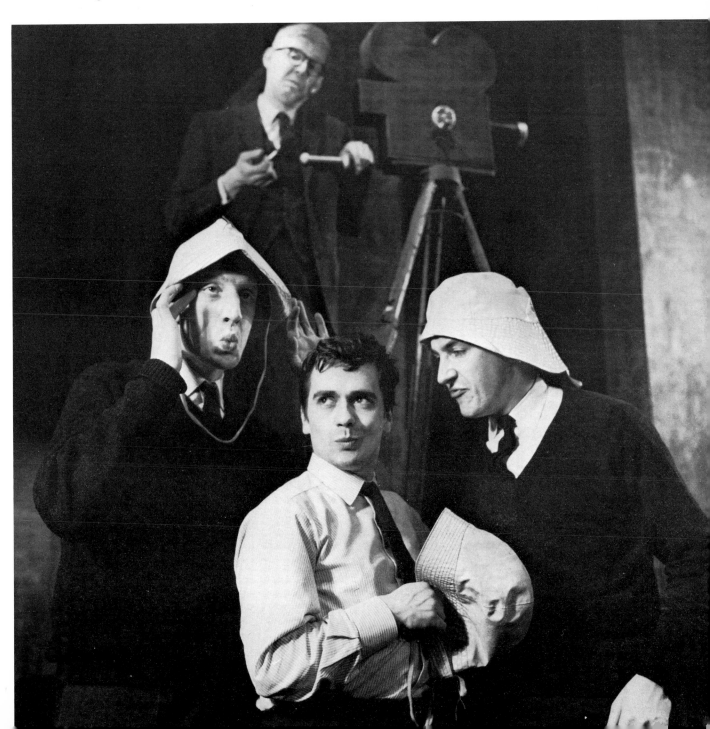

the launching of British television's first satirical cabaret caused a sensation. After just a few weeks, an audience numbering some twelve million was tuning in regularly to *That Was The Week That Was*. Under Sir Hugh Carlton Greene, Director General of the BBC – who had spent some time in Germany in the heyday of its Kabarett – a state television network for the first time created a programme based on current affairs which satirized political and social events.

Produced by Ned Sherrin, *TWTWTW* was a genuine television cabaret. Live studio audience and 'poor' cabaret stage were both brought to the at-home viewer through television cameras whose visibility and constant movement were as effective in breaking down small-screen illusion. as audience participation, an atmosphere of smoke and talk, had been in shattering the theatre's fictional fourth wall. Programmes included the satirical and jazz songs of Millicent Martin, a conférence of calculated blandness by the young David Frost, and sketches whose vitriolic wit was aimed at every aspect of the status quo, from royalty to the new trendy satirists themselves.

There might be Harold Macmillan making a stirring speech about the wonders of northern England, then catching the first train back to London. Or Prince Philip blithely claiming that although private education – that is public school – is only 2 per cent and leads to 82 per cent of the top jobs, this has got nothing to do with education . . . 'nor indeed have the public schools'. Or Field Marshal Lord Montgomery counselling a crowd of Manchester factory workers to imitate his example and not get married until the age of forty, since this was the key to success:

> Compared to a life on a martial crusade
> Marriage is just an effrontery
> Better by far than just getting laid
> Is to lay down your life for your country!

Or Bernard Levin discussing the Government's latest pamphlet on hints to house-holders in case of nuclear attack, and concluding that the suggested list of helpful items to be taken to the fall-out shelter – aspirins, bicarbonate of soda, teaspoons, vaseline – proved that the Government is 'under the impression that the unpleasantness of a nuclear attack will lie somewhere between that of a bad cold and a touch of indigestion'.

1963, the bleakest, certainly the coldest winter in England's recent history, saw strikes, large-scale unemployment, England's initial rejection from the Common Market, and the death of Labour leader Hugh Gaitskell. The times earned a grim critique from the *TWTWTW* team. As the year progressed, the series gradually lost its comic impulse and engaged in straightforward vituperative insult.

By the end of 1963, when Macmillan's resignation was two months past and the *TWTWTW* team had already lashed out savagely at his successor, the BBC announced that the series was to be terminated. The year's close also brought the end of The Establishment. The sixties boom in satire was over and while TV cabaret would find one form of survival in the zany surrealism of *Monty Python's Flying Circus*, it was not until the seventies merged into the eighties that the cabaret or club would serve again as a meeting place, a centre for laughter, invective and artistic experimentation.

Cabaret Lives!

In Britain it all began in 1979 with the return of a conservative government. Amidst the Soho strip clubs as the decade turned, cabarets sprang up in quick staccato succession: the Comedy Store, the Comic Strip, Cabaret Futura. They created and stimulated both an audience and performers, and the movement spread to the four corners of London. From Brixton to Archway, from Dalston to Notting Hill and beyond, to Bath, Bristol, the North, pubs, small theatres, college and concert halls were transformed into cabarets.

The new wave performers were fed in part by the aggression of punk. Indeed, they share one sector of their following with the pop music world. But the impetus for their quick-fire wit comes from the contradictions of the social and political arena, and from a government which speaks of putting the 'Great' back into Britain, of the heroism of belt-tightening, iron backbones, free enterprise, noble – perhaps even nuclear – wars, while the country is caught in a recessionary maelstrom.

'Recession,' quips self-styled Fat Bastard Alexei Sayle in one of his murderous throw-aways, 'is just a rumour put around by four million people without jobs.' 'There's a big sixties revival going on,' he adds, 'families living on eight quid a week. There's also a big thirties thing. You're no one unless you've got malnutrition.'

The comics who made their names in the Comedy Store and the Comic Strip – Keith Allen, Tony Allen, Jim Barclay, Rik Mayall, Andy de la Tour, Alexei Sayle, to name but a few – call themselves 'alternative'. Thus they differentiate themselves from conventional stand-up comedians with their repertoire of handbook jokes about the Irish, the Pakistanis or West Indians, nagging mother-in-laws and wives. But they also distinguish themselves from the university revue tradition which, since the days of *Beyond the Fringe*, has fed television and radio 'light entertainments'. Whereas the zany sketches and mad antics of the BBC's *Not the Nine O'Clock News* team are the eighties successors of TW^3 and *Monty Python*, the new wave comics, with their greater political astringency, trace a direct line back to Lenny Bruce whose acerbic monologues were self-scripted.

Alexei Sayle, son of working-class Liverpudlian communists, made his way through art school and a small Brecht troupe to the Comedy Store where he acted as compere. Strip club by day, the Comedy Store was set up on the model of its Los Angeles equivalent. Aspiring or established comics were booed, hissed, heckled off the tiny platform by an audience which was nothing if not interventionist. To survive

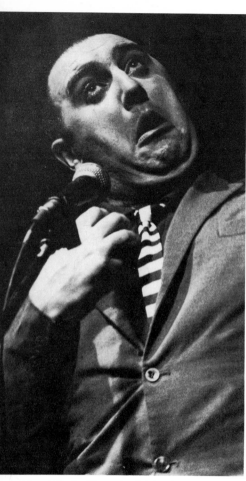

Alexei Sayle. Photo by Adrian Boot.

the 'gong' which guillotined acts in the Comedy Store was to hone one's wit and learn how to handle a live – and lively – critical public. A far cry, this, from the pre-packaging of television or the polite and captive theatre audience. It was here that Sayle, along with many others, polished his material before moving on to the Comic Strip and other venues.

Jaunty pork-pie hat rammed down over his eyes, his ripped-at-the-seams jacket tightly buttoned over an exaggerated corpulence, Sayle launches face and body into a series of clowning grotesqueries as pithy and rude as his language. His barbs fly and explode poisonously at government and police, mods, skinheads, and the liberal left, at poses and pretentions, whatever their social origins.

> . . . Yeah, I'm glad to be Cockney. I'm a genial Cockney bastard. Like the suit, John, do ya? I usually wear it with a kebab in the top pocket, yea, triffic, piss, bollocks, wanker. Just got me a grant from the Arts Council, wrote this poem didn't I? It's called Allo John, Got a New Motor? Triffic, yeah, bollocks, we don't give a stuff about Jean-Paul Sartre round our way, cos 'e knows fuck-all abaht the Cortina . . .'

The acute eye for style and stereotype informs all of Sayle's wit; whether it's the brash Cockney east-ender or the trendy lefty from a gentrified part of Stoke Newington whose middle-classness is evident from his Suzuki jeep – 'It's very important to have 4-wheel drive to go down to Sainsbury's' – as much as from the look of his house: 'You don't catch *them* living in the working class estates and talking about Chekhov and the Russian bourgeoisie in the windswept piazzas.'

> It's great Stoke Newington, actually. We've several very interesting kinds of cystitis going round. . . . It's great stuff this cystitis; in fact, we just formed a Cystitis Sufferers Against the Nazis. We had a march the other day. (Well, it was more of a mince, actually, going, 'ooh, fuck, ooh, aah, aah'. . .) I think it did a lot of good, you know. Actually the life style in Stoke Newington is terribly alternative, you know. I mean, everybody is growing their own denim, you know . . .

It is also in Stoke Newington that a new Youth Opportunities programme has been launched. It's called rioting. It creates lots of jobs for window glaziers.

Jim Barclay, who like so many of the new comedians comes out of political and fringe theatre, also takes a swipe at middle-class trendiness and pretension.

> Those New Year parties in Islington are wonderful, great. You turn up at the terraced house and there's a sign on the gate saying, 'Beware of the dog'. But it's been crossed out, and underneath they've written, 'Please be kind to our dog, he's only trying to come to terms with his naturally aggressive male tendencies'. And you go in, and there's the 10-year-old kid wearing hessian pyjamas and you ask him what he got for Christmas and he says, 'My parents don't recognize the patriarchal myth of Christmas imposed on us by capitalism; but

to celebrate the winter solstice I got a unisex, multi-racial Action Person from my mum and dad.'

Whereas the flavour of some of the new comics can be suggested on the page, others defy quotation altogether. Keith Allen's savage lambasting of the very fabric of society and of the most cherished of received ideas emerges only in the unfolding of a monologue in which the wit is caustically medicinal and confrontational. Though Allen's free-wheeling monologue and repartee can pack punches with the best of them ('I look up and I see the most extraordinary thing. There's this field full of horses, right. And here's the surprise – none of them's got policemen on.'), here humour takes second place to a process of illumination. In the best tradition of satire, one senses beneath Allen's dark comedy, a moral rigour, an idealist's force. In his 1983 alternative election broadcast, shown on Channel 4, Allen took on one of the many jarring personae at his disposal: a nightwatchman who, beneath the disturbingly neat, bewhiskered surface of a security guard, harbours a devastating view of contemporary Britain. The uniform of right wing petty-bourgeois respectability sets up false expectations, so that the ferocity of the anarchistic views, which the monologue then conveys hits home with all the more deadly accuracy to undermine a parliamentary system in which all parties are the same, equally locked in a game of international finance oblivious to the individual.

Though Keith Allen performed *The Nightwatchman* on television, he shares with many of the new wave comics a suspicion of a form which inevitably neutralises their material by taking it out of their control and re-presenting it as a commodity for mass consumption. Alexei Sayle states that he only appears on TV in order to gain a wider audience outside London for what is his true form, the cabaret act. Rik Mayall, one half of the 20th Century Coyote team, a staple of the Comic Strip, created the character of Kevin Turvey, TV Reporter of the Year, in order, he claims, to waste TV time, a commodity which is rarely meant to be squandered. And Tony Allen, veteran of the Comedy Store and the Comic Strip, one of the originators of the group which banded together under the banner of Alternative Cabaret, has made more sortees into Speakers' Corner than into television.

Although under long-time socialist comedian Roland Muldoon, public subsidy has gone into the creation of political cabaret, particularly evenings against nuclear power, many of the radical comics see subsidy as anathema. Indeed, Tony Allen, playwright and one of the founders of the fringe Rough Theatre, states provocatively that subsidy has in part been responsible for keeping fringe, as well as more established theatrical forms, alive beyond their allotted time. If audiences had had to choose, if economics had determined style, then cabaret would have burgeoned in 1972. His Alternative Cabaret, which travels the country, brings together new wave comedians, performers and musicians 'to present non-racist, non-sexist entertainment which undoubtedly will precipitate the downfall of capitalism and bring an end to injustice and tyranny wherever it rears its ugly head'.

These grandiose claims bear more than a tinge of irony. Nevertheless, it is true that by linking up with bands such as the vehement Poison Girls, Alternative Cabaret brings entertainment with a serious, if not overtly educative, intent to youthful audiences who might not normally be receptive to the naked word. Tony Allen has had many a beer can flung at him, but therein lies part of the challenge of the new wave performers: to capture the attention of an aggressive young public, illuminate attitudes and generate shifts of perception amongst skinheads, punks, mods and a variety of sub-cultural groups.

Tall, thin, curly-haired, with something of the bearing of a latter-day Karl Valentin crossed with a street player, Tony Allen – 'voted Ladbroke Grove's best-dressed squatter three years running' – engages his public quietly and speaks to them directly.

Tony Allen. Photo by Tim Malyon.

> Anyway, there was this drunk, homosexual Pakistani squatter who takes my mother-in-law to an Irish restaurant and he says to the West Indian waiter, 'Waiter, there's a racial stereotype in my soup,' and the waiter says, 'What d'you expect for 40p – a Caucasian stockbroker?'...

Tony Allen's monologue is political: 'The American's have a new research programme for developing a device that wipes out arguments against nuclear weapons but leaves apathy intact'. But increasingly he has dealt with the difficult area of sexual politics, taking himself as subject and earnestly defining a trajectory which illuminates macho attitudes, advertising imagery and society's complicity with rape. There is, in the very quiet casualness of Allen's delivery and the immediacy of his contact with his audience, something which is at the heart of contemporary cabaret: a negation of the conventional link between public and performer which makes the first a passive consumer of the latter's pre-packaged product.

It is significant that amongst the new wave comics, few – with the exception of the talented singer-raconteuses, Sharon Landau, Maggie Steed and Pauline Melville – are women. The sexist bias of so much traditional comedy, the difficulty women have of speaking publicly in their own, rather than a character's voice, the charged values attached to the particular 'look' a woman has on stage – all make for numerous problems for the female comic. Interestingly, various performance and video artists have made this whole tangled nexus of roles and relations the very subject of their work.

Amongst the host of musicians, singers, comics, sketch groups, performance and video artists, jugglers, belly dancers, manifesto readers and fire eaters to find their way onto the cabaret platform in recent years, one group deserves special attention both for its links with the origins of cabaret and for the size of its following: the new wave and punk poets – Attilla the Stockbroker, Benjamin Zephaniah, Joolz, Seething Wells, to name but a few. All owe something to John Cooper Clarke whose rapid-fire verse paved the way for spoken poetry in rock venues, but also bear a loose affinity with the jazz-poetry experiments of Adrian Mitchell and Christopher Logue. Whereas the dark comedians often have a following in the very middle class they lampoon,

186

the new wave poets find their audiences and their origins – perhaps because the poetry establishment is assiduously tied to the page – in the rock and punk youth cultures.

'What we have done,' says Seething Wells, clad in the paraphernalia which designates him a skinhead, 'is to reinstate verse as a form of oral entertainment instead of intellectual masturbation'. Beneath the skinhead garb which points his identity with a particular sector of angry, disenfranchised youth, there is a serious intent. The style allows him to speak directly about politics, macho attitudes, racial prejudices, to a group whose ears might otherwise be closed. Although he is a socialist, that makes him quite unlike labour politicians who, he says, have no links to youth whatsoever. Seething Wells sees himself as an alternative newsreader, a propagandist, willing to use any of the tools showbiz has learned over the years. During the Falklands War, he delivered the following withering blast in machine-gun tempo.

Seething Wells.

> News at ten used to be boring
> Test tube babies, Maggie spreading rabies
> Unemployment, Northern Ireland
> But never any REAL VIOLENCE
> But now its NEW! IMPROVED! News at Ten
> Alistair Burnett goes Grecian 2000
> with the NEW! ADDED! FALKLANDS! ingredient
> 8 out of 10 dictators recommended
> There's nowt like a full-scale war
> For sending workers off to bed
> With thoughts of ENGLAND in their cloth-capped heads
> Tabloid editors spurting lies
> Benny Hill writes the headlines
> 'STICK IT UP YOUR JUNTA!'
> Page 3 is on page 5
> 'Cos it's more fun wanking over guns and bombs
> Than placidly smiling platinum blondes
> It's a quick wargasm
> A war on the cheap
> Save the penguin! Save the sheep!
> Save the Falklands! Smash the Fascists!
> And their BRITISH-trained pilots in their BRITISH-built jets
> And their BRITISH-built warships
> Sold to them by the very same brainless fat-gutted Tory shits
> Who blandly bleat CRUSADE AGAINST THE FASCISTS!
> Well I'm into crusades now and then
> So let's start with the bastards who lurk in No. 10
> But no, it's wheel out the Spitfires, revive Vera Lynn
> It's the spirit of the Blitz until they bring back rationing
> And conscript a garrison of 10 million women and men
> Till the next time they decide it's time again
> For fresh blood on News at Ten.

187

Richard Strange and Rene Eyre.
Photo by Perry Ogden.

Of all the cabarets to spring up in Britain over recent years, it is Soho's Cabaret Futura, the brain-child of Richard Strange, which bears most atmospheric resemblance to its Weimar kin. Indeed, as Strange has pinpointed, the links between the thirties and the eighties are not imaginary: 'the re-emergence of international anti-semitism, massive unemployment and rearmament and, balanced against that, people dressing up and the cult of decadence'.

Richard Strange's intention was to create a club which was as much a social space as an aesthetic space, to blur the distinction between audience and performers, and to mix not only the kinds of audiences – the art world with the rock world – but the genres themselves – dance, music, performance, sketches, comic monologue, film, recitation and video art. In the event Cabaret Futura became an overnight success and when several hundred disappointed punters a night had to be turned away from its initial tiny venue, the cabaret moved into more spacious Wardour Street premises. Strange accounts for the success by pointing to the social moment: one of creative excitement when people were coming out of the ethos of destructive punk nihilism and saying that art was no longer a dirty word. Cabaret Futura became the focus and meeting place for the energy which fed the explosion in fashion, photography, filmmaking and music. More than that, it suggested a reaction to television, the growing demand for a live venue to serve specific, not standardized mass tastes. But success is a two-edged sword and as Cabaret Futura was transformed into a locus for the fashionable, a place to be seen in and to be reported on in the gossip columns, Strange felt that the fine balance between performer and spectator had been tipped and he closed the venue. Late in 1982, after a tour of the cabaret in the USA, he opened a new cabaret, The Slammer, which he designated as an artotheque, 'a regular, sympathetic space where performers are being judged as working, developing artists, not as hip novelties on the Rock Circuit nor as precious icons of the "serious" art/dance circuit, nor even as potential fodder for Channel 4 arts programmes.'

Formerly of the proto-punk band, Doctors of Madness, Richard Strange gives to his own performance a rare energy as he flings his tall, thin, loose-limbed figure about the stage with demonic abandon. He performs mostly solo over pre-recorded backup tapes – which makes travelling from venue to venue more efficient – to a background of slides and often with a dancer. A night at the Cabaret Futura would usually end with the nattily stylish Strange unleashing a number or more from his concept rock work, *The Phenomenal Rise of Richard Strange*. This recounts the story of a rock star who colludes with big business and media to become the president of a United Europe. But accession to power leads to a concern with social justice, the redistribution of wealth. The powers that instated him turn against him. Assassination of the man, or ambiguously of the media myth, is then inevitable. More recently, Strange, as a haunting, slightly sinister Sigmund Freud, has been performing his surreal adaptation of the introductory poem from D. M. Thomas's best-selling novel, *The White Hotel*.

It was while he was touring the USA as a 'one-man show with Revox' and moving out of the standard rock conveyor-belt circuit that Richard Strange was inspired to start a cabaret. For the Manhattan axis provided precisely that cross-fertilisation between popular culture and 'serious' art, that mixing of various kinds of public which is seminal to cabaret. New wave clubs, with post-punk funk music and outlandish leather and hair fashion at their core, had been part of Manhattan's ever style-conscious social life since CBGB's became, in 1975, downtown's answer to the Lincoln Centre. The Mudd Club, the Danceteria, the Peppermint Lounge and a score of SoHo and Tribec bars surfaced in its wake and served as meeting places and performance venues for artists as diverse in range as William Burroughs and Bow Wow Wow, Marianne Faithful and Laurie Anderson, Glenn Branca and Peter Gordon with his new music, rock fusion band. If the impetus to Cabaret in London had come from the alternative comics and satire, then in New York it was the merger of the experimental avant-garde in the visual arts and music with the rock club scene which fostered cabaret New York-style. Difficult though it might be to imagine as serious a composer as Philip Glass playing in a space which simultaneously caters to a DJ and a dancing public, the mix is perhaps no stranger than that which took place in the Paris heyday of the twenties and Le Boeuf sur le toit.

Of the many artists who have performed in the American clubs, few engage in the satirical thrust of the British new wave, perhaps because American reality defiantly outstrips satire. Comics on the whole are tied into the traditional night club circuit and if they make it to Los Angeles's Comedy Store, then the ambition is to appear on television. There is, however, one exception. Eric Bogosian moved out of performance-art mixed-media work to create what he calls 'amplified solos', breakneck monologues which journey through a dismal American landscape of types, from bums, pimps and dealers to sinister middle-class mafiosi, torture merchants and TV preachers; or capture the radio voices of America in a blast of slogans, jingles, ads and disasters of escalating horror. The precision of Bogosian's performance as he launches himself with rare intensity into his various roles, the nightmare vision he presents of a death-obsessed America, link him more closely with a Keith Allen than any of the American stand-up comics.

Many of the artists who perform in the New York clubs have had some links with the Kitchen, an experimental performing and mixed media art centre in SoHo. But as Jim Fourrat, manager of the Danceteria claims, at the Kitchen whatever passed on stage was treated with reverence or simply endurance. Put the art into a place where 'people get drunk, get laid, pass out or go home, have fights, get bored' like the Mudd Club or the Danceteria and 'the artists have to fight to capture the audience'. This, he feels, makes for better art and for better audience-performer communication. Fourrat sees the clubs not only as laboratory and testing ground for the artists, but also as a place where audiences who would never venture into an art centre are given the opportunity of seeing something which is not a homogenized mass product. '. . . this is a place that presents itself as a serious alternative to mass culture. It does say to the person whose only choice is mass culture that he can go here and have a good time and have it different'.

Eric Bogosian. Photo by Jo Bonney.

Performance in the SoHo clubs moves across traditional genres with a kaleidoscopic ease. Curators are occasionally brought in to assemble particular shows or evenings. The flavour of a cabaret scene where forms and publics blend is suggested by Edit Deak's *Dubbed in Glamour* evenings in 1980, described in terms which bear a kinship to a Dada manifesto:

> . . . three long nights of fun, extravagance and spectacle, including new-new-new wave rock, funk hip hop and post-post-post modernist entertainments, readings by glitterati literati. These rites of personality cult are dedicated to the average American in search of self-image (and are) an exposé of the energies of the Para-SoHo luminaries, that part of the art-world which never had a loft, is younger than the art-world, and hangs out in Clubs.

If New York's heady mixture of clubs and art bears the imprint of Manhattan's self-obsession with the latest fashion a little too blatantly, it is nonetheless the envy of many artists on the other side of the Atlantic. In Britain, the divisions between conventional art forms and between popular and 'serious' audiences are far more rigid, though experiments in performance and dance theatre, such as those seen at the Institute of Contemporary Arts in recent years, or the existence of cabaret even within the bastion of the National Theatre, suggest that cross-fertilization is not impossible. Certainly, the European avant-garde from Mayakovsky to Brecht, from Dada through Picasso to Surrealism has variously fed off popular forms, mixed the conventional genres and attempted to find new audiences. It is not surprising that today the stimulus to original experiment should come from the rock world or the new sound and video technologies.

Given the pressures of the political and economic climate, the looming threat of nuclear war, it is equally apparent why artists and performers should seek more direct and unedited contact with their audiences. The revival of cabaret is an ambivalent symptom. It points to the fact that the decade cries out for the astringent edge of satire. Even if, as history has all-too-clearly shown, satire cannot stem the tides of disaster, that the artist's gun is no particularly potent weapon, it can instigate shifts of awareness, indicate that other potential reality which is the home of hope. Brecht's wry smile hovers over the satirist's domain: 'I could do but little, but the rulers would have sat safer had I not been. I hope.'

Beyond that, the revival of cabaret signals a new energy in the creative sphere. For where else – in an epoch of multinational TV and music packaging – but in a crowded, smoke-filled cabaret, can audiences gather in intimate groups rather than as statistical mass? Where else can they cross the threshold from passive spectatorship to participation? jump the divide between serious 'art to be endured' and entertainment? and fling away the straitjacket of formal conventions? And so cabaret lives again as a meeting place, an artistic laboratory and a locus for aggressive, new wave satire.

Index

Figure numbers in italics refer to illustration pages.